Exercise Technique Manual for Resistance Training

SECOND EDITION

Exercise Technique Manual for Resistance Training

SECOND EDITION

National Strength and Conditioning Association

Human Kinetics

Library of Congress Cataloging-in-Publication Data

Exercise technique manual for resistance training / National Strength and Conditioning Association. -- 2nd ed.
　　p. cm.
　Rev. ed. of: Exercise Technique Checklist Manual : A Review of Free Weight and Machine Resistance Training Exercises, published in 1997 by the NSCA Certification Commission.
　　ISBN-13: 978-0-7360-7127-7 (soft cover)
　　ISBN-10: 0-7360-7127-X (soft cover)
　　1. Weight training. 2. Free weights. 3. Exercise. 4. Personal trainers. I. National Strength & Conditioning Association (U.S.). II. Title: Exercise Technique Checklist Manual.
　　GV546.E96 2008
　　613.7′1--dc22

2007047356

ISBN-10: 0-7360-7127-X
ISBN-13: 978-0-7360-7127-7

This book is a revised edition of *Exercise Technique Checklist Manual: A Review of Free Weight and Machine Resistance Training Exercises*, published in 1997 by the NSCA Certification Commission.

Acquisitions Editor: Michael S. Bahrke, PhD; **Developmental Editor:** Christine M. Drews; **Assistant Editor:** Katherine Maurer; **Copyeditor:** Jan Feeney; **Proofreader:** Jim Burns; **Graphic Designer:** Bob Reuther; **Graphic Artist:** Angela K. Snyder; **Cover Designer:** Keith Blomberg; **Photographer (cover):** Neil Bernstein; **Photographer (interior):** Neil Bernstein; **Visual Production Assistant:** Joyce Brumfield; **Photo Office Assistant:** Jason Allen; **Printer:** Sheridan Books

This book was edited by Roger Earle, MA; CSCS,*D; NSCA-CPT,*D, and Nolan Harms, MS; CSCS,*D; NSCA-CPT,*D. The editors thank Creighton University in Omaha, Nebraska, for providing the location for the photo shoot for this book. Specific thanks go to Satoshi Ochi, MA; CSCS,*D; NSCA-CPT,*D, Creighton's head strength and conditioning coach, who was instrumental in preparing for and running the photo shoot.

Printed in the United States of America　　20　19　18　17　16　15　14

The paper in this book is certified under a sustainable forestry program.

Human Kinetics
Web site: www.HumanKinetics.com

United States: Human Kinetics, P.O. Box 5076, Champaign, IL 61825-5076
800-747-4457
e-mail: humank@hkusa.com

Canada: Human Kinetics, 475 Devonshire Road Unit 100, Windsor, ON N8Y 2L5
800-465-7301 (in Canada only)
e-mail: info@hkcanada.com

Europe: Human Kinetics, 107 Bradford Road, Stanningley, Leeds LS28 6AT, United Kingdom
+44 (0) 113 255 5665
e-mail: hk@hkeurope.com

Australia: Human Kinetics, 57A Price Avenue, Lower Mitcham, South Australia 5062
08 8372 0999
e-mail: info@hkaustralia.com

New Zealand: Human Kinetics, P.O. Box 80, Torrens Park, South Australia 5062
0800 222 062
e-mail: info@hknewzealand.com

E4205

Contents

DVD Menu

Preface

This manual was developed by the National Strength and Conditioning Association (NSCA) primarily for those preparing for the Certified Strength and Conditioning Specialist or NSCA-Certified Personal Trainer examinations. Those who are studying for NSCA Certification examinations will find the use of this manual in conjunction with the DVDs especially helpful in preparing for exam questions relating to anatomy, biomechanics, program design (e.g., exercise selection), and exercise technique.

Exercise Technique Manual for Resistance Training, Second Edition, also serves as an excellent resource for strength and conditioning professionals, health fitness instructors, and personal trainers using resistance training exercises in their own programs or when instructing others. College and university faculty and students will find that this manual and the DVDs complement hands-on instruction and aid in teaching exercise technique without requiring the use of a weight room.

This manual describes proper technique for 37 free-weight and 20 machine exercises. The exercise technique checklists identify the primary muscle groups involved and the correct grip, stance, body position, and range of motion for each exercise. Additionally, descriptions of joint actions, spotting suggestions, and tips for avoiding injury are provided.

Although the exercise technique checklists were written by experts, no one should attempt to perform a new exercise without the supervision of a certified strength and conditioning professional or NSCA-certified personal trainer. It is also recommended that anyone considering participating in an exercise program consult a physician before beginning the program.

For more information on other CSCS or NSCA-CPT exam preparation materials, please contact the NSCA toll-free at 800-815-6826/ 719-632-6722 for calls from outside the United States) or visit www.nsca-lift.org.

Introduction

This manual describes proper technique for 37 free-weight and 20 machine exercises that are categorized into the following groups:

- Power and explosive (total body)
- Hip and thigh (multijoint and single joint)
- Calf (single joint)
- Chest (multijoint and single joint)
- Back (multijoint and single joint)
- Shoulder (multijoint and single joint)
- Biceps (single joint)
- Triceps (single joint)
- Forearm (single joint)
- Abdomen

The exercises are also shown on the accompanying DVDs, and icons indicate which of the two DVDs shows the exercises in that section.

Multijoint exercises involve two or more joints that change angles during the execution of a repetition (e.g., the hip, knee, and ankle joints during the power clean). Single-joint exercises allow movement in only one joint during a repetition (e.g., the elbow joint during the biceps curl exercise). For the purposes of this manual, the joints of the shoulder girdle are combined with the true (glenohumeral) shoulder joint and, therefore, treated as one joint. For example, the barbell pullover and the lateral shoulder raise exercises are labeled as single-joint movements, despite the obvious involvement of several shoulder girdle joints in addition to the glenohumeral joint. Additionally, only the predominant muscles are included. While many other muscles may assist during the exercise or may function as stabilizers, they are not included in the Muscular Involvement charts.

Each of the exercise descriptions in this manual includes details about the following:

- Type of exercise (i.e., multijoint or single joint)
- Description of the concentric action of movement
- Muscle group or body area affected
- Predominant muscle groups and muscles involved
- Guidelines for proper exercise technique listed in the order that they are to be performed
- Which exercises require a spotter (as designated by a 🖐)

Spotting Guidelines

The exercise movements that require the use of a spotter fulfill these criteria:

- A bar or dumbbells move over the head or face.
- A bar is placed on the back or neck or is racked at (i.e., positioned on) the front of the shoulders or clavicles.

Power and explosive exercises are *not* spotted. When using a spotter, the lifter must communicate with the spotter about bar liftoff or racking signals and the desired amount and method of assistance *before* beginning a set.

General Safety Suggestions

Follow these guidelines to ensure safe exercise technique:

- Perform power and explosive exercises in a clean, dry, flat, well-marked area (e.g., on a lifting platform) free of obstacles and people. This guideline can also apply to other complex nonpower exercises such as the lunge, deadlift, and step-up. (Note: Some photographs of power exercises show the person standing sideways—rotated 90 degrees—on the lifting platform. This position was used *only* to capture the photo of the exercise. The correct position is where the weight plates are placed on the rubberized sections rather than the wooden sections of the platform.)
- If a repetition in a power and explosive exercise cannot be completed, push forward on the bar to move the body backward and let the bar fall to the floor. **Do not attempt to "save" a missed or failed repetition of this type of exercise.**
- Before performing exercises that finish with the bar overhead, check to see if there is sufficient floor-to-ceiling space.
- Use a bar with revolving sleeves, especially for the power and explosive exercises.
- Use a squat or power rack with the supporting pins or hooks set to position the bar at armpit height for the front squat and back squat; also use that setting when beginning or ending an exercise with the bar at shoulder height is preferred to beginning or ending on the floor.
- When lifting the bar up and out of the supporting pins or hooks of a squat or power rack in preparation for an exercise, always step *backward* at the *beginning* of the set and step *forward* at the *end* of the set. **Do not walk backward to return the bar to the rack**.
- Always use collars and locks to secure free-weight plates on the bar.
- Fully insert the selectorized pin or key (usually L or T shaped) into the weight stack for machine exercises.

Preparatory Body Position and Lifting Guidelines

Often a lifter needs to lift a bar or dumbbells off the floor before getting into the starting position of an exercise (e.g., bent-over row, biceps curl, flat or incline dumbbell bench press or fly, upright row, lying barbell triceps extension, stiff-leg deadlift). To avoid excessive strain on the low back, place the body in the correct position to lift the weight safely and effectively.

First, use the correct stance in relation to the bar or dumbbells *and* properly grasp the bar or dumbbell handles:

- Squat down behind the bar or between the dumbbells.
- Place the feet between hip- and shoulder-width apart.
- If lifting a bar, position the bar close to the shins and over the balls of the feet and grasp the bar with a closed grip that is shoulder-width (or slightly wider) apart.
- If lifting dumbbells, stand directly between them and grasp the handles with a closed grip and a neutral arm or hand position.
- Position the arms outside the knees with the elbows extended.

Follow these six steps to place the body in the correct preparatory position *before* lifting a weight off the floor. The following guidelines also describe how the body should be positioned immediately before the first repetition of a power exercise (e.g., snatch, power clean):

1. The back is flat or slightly arched.
2. The trapezius is relaxed and slightly stretched, the chest is held up and out, and the shoulder blades are held together.
3. The head is in line with the spine or slightly hyperextended.
4. The body's weight is balanced between the middle and balls of the feet, but the heels are in contact with the floor.
5. The shoulders are over or slightly in front of the bar.
6. The eyes are focused straight ahead or slightly upward.

To avoid frequent repetition, the checklists for many of the 57 exercises in this manual refer to this six-item list of instructions as "preparatory body position and lifting guidelines," but the full list is not provided for each exercise.

Weight Belt Recommendations

The use of a weight belt can contribute to injury-free training. Its appropriateness is based on the type of exercise *and* the relative load lifted. If a weight belt is worn, it is most appropriate to do so in these situations:

- During exercises that place stress on the low back (e.g., back squat, front squat, deadlift)
- During sets with near-maximal or maximal loads

Both conditions should exist; it is not necessary, for example, to wear a weight belt when lifting lighter loads even when performing an exercise that places stress on the low back. This strategy may reduce the risk of injuries to the low back, but only when combined with correct exercise technique and proper spotting. Note that some people may have increased blood pressure as a result of wearing a weight belt. Elevated blood pressure is associated with dizziness and fatigue and could result in headaches, fainting, or injury. Additionally, it is recommended that people with hypertension or any preexisting cardiovascular condition not wear a weight belt because doing so might lead to a heart attack or stroke.

Breathing Guidelines

The best general guideline about proper breathing during a resistance training exercise is to exhale through the sticking point (the most difficult part of the exercise) of the concentric (exertion) phase and inhale during the easier part of the exercise (eccentric phase). Typically, the sticking point occurs soon after the transition from the eccentric phase to the concentric phase. For example, the sticking point of the free-weight bench press exercise occurs about halfway through the upward movement phase. At that point, the lifter should exhale through this portion of the movement. As the bar is lowered back down to the chest, the lifter should inhale. This breathing strategy applies to nearly all resistance training exercises.

For additional breathing guidelines, including more about performing the Valsalva maneuver, refer to *Essentials of Strength Training and Conditioning* or *NSCA's Essentials of Personal Training*.

TOTAL BODY

Power and Explosive Exercises

DVD 1

Name	Description of the concentric action	PREDOMINANT MUSCLES INVOLVED	
		Muscle group or body area	Muscles
Snatch	Hip extension	Gluteals	Gluteus maximus
		Hamstrings	Semimembranosus Semitendinosus Biceps femoris
	Knee extension	Quadriceps	Vastus lateralis Vastus intermedius Vastus medialis Rectus femoris
	Ankle plantar flexion	Calf	Soleus Gastrocnemius
	Shoulder flexion and abduction	Shoulders	Anterior and medial deltoids
	Shoulder girdle elevation	Upper shoulder and upper back	Trapezius (upper portion)
	Elbow extension	Upper arm (posterior)	Triceps brachii
Power clean	Same as snatch, but the concentric action does not include elbow extension		
Hang clean	Same as snatch, but the concentric action does not include elbow extension		
Push press	Same as snatch except there is greater shoulder flexion and abduction (anterior and medial deltoids) and greater elbow extension (triceps brachii)		
Push jerk	Same as snatch		

TOTAL BODY

Snatch

From the starting position, this exercise involves lifting the bar overhead with the arms fully extended—all in one movement. Although the upward movement phase consists of four distinct phases, the upward movement of the bar occurs in one *continuous* motion.

Starting Position

☐ Stand with the feet placed between hip- and shoulder-width apart with the toes pointed slightly outward so the knees track directly over the feet.

☐ Squat down with the hips lower than the shoulders and grasp the bar evenly with a pronated grip. The hand placement on the bar is wider than it is for other exercises. It can be estimated by measuring the distance from the knuckles' edge of a clenched fist of an arm extended out to the side and parallel to the floor, across the back of the arm and upper back, to the outside edge of the opposite shoulder. Alternatively, the lifter's grip width can be estimated by measuring the elbow-to-elbow distance when the upper arms are abducted directly out from the sides and parallel to the floor. This distance is the space

**Grip measurement:
Fist to opposite shoulder**

**Grip measurement:
Elbow to elbow**

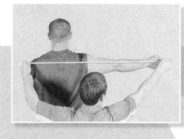

Starting position

First pull

between the hands when they are grasping the bar. If necessary, this spacing can be modified depending on shoulder flexibility and arm length. The actual grip can be a closed grip or a hook grip. To use a hook grip, place a pronated hand on the bar and first wrap the thumb around the bar, then wrap the four fingers. The first one or two fingers, depending on their length, will cover the thumb. This grip is effective for lifting maximal or near-maximal loads, but it can be uncomfortable initially. Wrapping the thumbs with athletic tape will alleviate the pressure when using the hook grip.

☐ Position the arms outside the knees with the elbows fully extended and pointing out to the sides.

☐ Position the bar approximately 1 inch (3 cm) in front of the shins and over the balls of the feet.

☐ Just before liftoff, observe the preparatory body position and lifting guidelines (see introduction) to place the body in the correct position to lift the bar off the floor. All repetitions begin from this position.

☐ Exact positions of the torso, hips, knees, and bar are dependent on an individual's segment lengths and lower-body joint flexibility. An inflexible person attempting to get into the correct starting position of the snatch may have difficulty grasping the bar with the elbows extended while keeping the heels on the floor. If the preparatory body position cannot be achieved, the hang snatch is an alternative because it does not require the lifter to start with the bar on the floor. It instead begins with the bar above the knees.

Scoop   **End of the second pull**   **Catch**

First Pull

The portion of the upward movement phase from liftoff to where the bar is just above the knees is termed the *first pull*.

☐ Begin the exercise by forcefully extending the hips and knees. These joints must extend at the same rate to keep the back and torso angle constant in relation to the floor. Do not let the hips rise before or faster than the shoulders. Maintaining the flat (or slightly arched) back position while shifting balance slowly from over the middle of the feet toward the heels helps in maintaining a consistent torso angle.

☐ The elbows should still be fully extended, the head neutral in relation to the spine, and the shoulders over or slightly ahead of the bar.

☐ As the bar is raised, it should be kept as close to the shins as possible; slightly shifting the body's weight back toward the heels as the bar is lifted will promote proper bar trajectory.

Transition (Scoop)

The portion of the ascent where the knees and thighs move forward under the bar is called the *transition* or *scoop*.

☐ As the bar rises to just above the knees, thrust the hips forward and slightly re-flex the knees to move the thighs against and the knees under the bar.

☐ During this second knee bend, the body's weight shifts forward toward the balls of the feet, but the heels remain in contact with the floor.

☐ Keep the back flat or slightly arched, the elbows fully extended and pointed out to the sides, and the head in line with the spine.

☐ The shoulders should still be over the bar, although they will tend to move backward as the knees and thighs are scooped under the bar. The body is in the "power position" at the end of this phase.

Second Pull (Power Phase)

The upward movement from the power position with the bar at the thighs and close to the body to where the lower-body joints are fully extended and the bar has reached its maximum velocity is referred to as the *second pull* or *power phase*.

☐ The bar should be near to or in contact with the front of the thighs above the knees. Initiate a fast upward jumping motion by quickly extending the hips, knees, and ankles. Note that ankle extension here (and in the descriptions for all of the power exercises) refers to plantar flexion.

☐ The bar should pass as close to the body as possible.

☐ Maintain a torso position with the back flat or slightly arched, the elbows pointing out to the sides, and the head in line with the spine.

☐ Keep the shoulders over the bar and the elbows extended as long as possible while the hips, knees, and ankles are extending.

☐ As the lower-body joints fully extend, rapidly shrug the shoulders upward. The elbows should be extended and pointing out to the sides during the shrugging movement.

☐ As the shoulders reach their highest elevation, flex the elbows to begin pulling the body under the bar. The upper-body movements are similar to the upright row exercise, only with a wider grip. The elbows move up and out to the sides.

☐ Continue to pull with the arms as high and as long as possible.

☐ Because of the jumping effort of the lower body and the pulling effort of the upper body, the torso will be erect or slightly hyperextended, the head will be tilted slightly back, and the feet may lose contact with the floor.

Catch

The act of receiving the bar in the overhead position is called the *catch* phase of the snatch.

☐ After the lower body has fully extended and the bar reaches near-maximal height, the body is pulled under the bar by rotating the arms and hands around then under the bar and by flexing the hips and knees into approximately a quarter-squat position.

☐ The feet typically regain contact with the floor in a slightly wider stance and with the toes pointed out slightly farther than at the initial position.

☐ Once the arms are under the bar, extend the elbows quickly to push the bar up and the body downward under the bar.

☐ The bar should be caught over and slightly behind the head with
   ■ fully extended elbows,
   ■ an erect and tight torso,
   ■ a neutral head position,
   ■ flat feet, and
   ■ the body's weight over the middle of the feet.

☐ Ideally, the quarter-squat position will be reached with the elbows extended just as the bar reaches its maximum height.

☐ After gaining control and balance, stand up by extending the hips and knees to a fully erect position.

Downward Movement

☐ If rubber bumper plates are used, the bar can be returned to the floor with a controlled drop; the bounce of the plates should be controlled with the hands on or near the bar.

☐ Most commonly, the bar is lowered slowly from the overhead position by gradually reducing the muscular tension of the upper body to allow a controlled descent of the bar to the thighs. The hips and knees are simultaneously flexed to cushion the impact of the bar on the thighs. The bar is then lowered by squatting down until it touches the floor.

☐ Reposition the bar and the body for the next repetition, if applicable.

Power Clean

This exercise is similar to the snatch with two major differences:

1. The final bar position is at the shoulders, not over the head.
2. The grip is approximately shoulder-width apart, whereas the snatch has a considerably wider grip.

Because of the many commonalities, the description of the power clean technique is slightly abbreviated and emphasis is placed on the unique aspects of this exercise in comparison to the snatch.

Starting Position

☐ Stand with the feet placed between hip- and shoulder-width apart with the toes pointed slightly outward so the knees track directly over the feet.

☐ Squat down with the hips lower than the shoulders and grasp the bar evenly with a shoulder-width (or slightly wider), pronated grip.

☐ Position the arms outside the knees with the elbows fully extended and pointing out to the sides.

Starting position   **First pull**

☐ Position the bar approximately 1 inch (3 cm) in front of the shins and over the balls of the feet.

☐ Just before liftoff, observe the preparatory body position and lifting guidelines (see introduction) to place the body in the correct position to lift the bar off the floor. All repetitions begin from this position.

☐ Exact positions of the torso, hips, knees, and bar are related to body segment length and lower-body joint flexibility. An alternative exercise is the hang clean (see page 12) that begins with the bar just above the knees instead of on the floor.

First Pull

☐ Begin the exercise by forcefully extending the hips and knees. Keep the back or torso angle constant in relation to the floor; do not let the hips rise before or faster than the shoulders, and keep the back flat or slightly arched.

☐ Maintain full elbow extension, with the head neutral in relation to the spine, and the shoulders over or slightly ahead of the bar.

☐ Keep the bar as close to the shins as possible.

| **Scoop** | **Middle of the second pull** | **Catch** |

Transition (Scoop)

☐ As the bar rises to just above the knees, thrust the hips forward and slightly re-flex the knees to move the thighs against and the knees under the bar.

☐ As the knees re-flex, shift the body's weight forward toward the balls of the feet, keeping the heels on the floor.

☐ Maintain a flat or slightly arched back, with the elbows fully extended and pointing out to the sides, the shoulders over or slightly ahead of the bar, and the head neutral in relation to the spine.

☐ At the finish of the scoop, the body is in position for the second pull (power phase).

Second Pull (Power Phase)

☐ From this position with the bar on the thighs between the knees and middle of the thighs, start the second pull by forcefully and quickly extending the hips, knees, and ankles.

☐ The bar should pass as close to the torso as possible.

☐ Keep the shoulders over the bar and the elbows extended as long as possible while the hips, knees, and ankles are extending.

☐ As the lower-body joints fully extend, rapidly shrug the shoulders upward. The elbows should be kept extended and pointing out to the sides during the shrugging movement.

☐ As the shoulders reach their highest elevation, flex the elbows to begin pulling the body under the bar.

☐ Continue to pull with the arms as high and as long as possible with the elbows moving up and out to the sides.

☐ The upward momentum from the jumping motion will result in an erect or slightly hyperextended torso and head, and the feet may come up off the floor.

Catch

The catch phase of the power clean ends with the bar on the anterior deltoids and clavicles, similar to the arm and bar position of the front squat exercise.

☐ As the second pull ends with the bar at maximal height, pull the body under the bar by rotating the arms and hands around then under the bar and re-flex the hips and knees to approximately a quarter-squat position.

☐ The feet will recontact the floor in a slightly wider stance in comparison to the starting position.

☐ The bar should be caught at the anterior deltoids and clavicles with the
  - ▪ head facing forward,
  - ▪ neck neutral or slightly hyperextended,
  - ▪ wrists hyperextended,
  - ▪ elbows fully flexed,

- ■ upper arms parallel to the floor,
- ■ back flat or slightly arched,
- ■ feet flat on the floor, and
- ■ body's weight over the middle of the feet.

☐ The bar should be caught with the torso almost fully erect and the shoulders slightly ahead of the buttocks. This position, which parallels the body position during the beginning of the downward movement phase of the front squat, allows for the bar to be directly over the center of gravity.

☐ If the torso is too erect, the momentum of the bar will push the shoulders backward and hyperextend the low back, resulting in an increased risk of injury.

☐ After gaining control and balance, stand up to a fully erect position.

Downward Movement

☐ At the completion of the repetition, rotate the arms back around the bar to "unrack" it from the anterior deltoids and clavicles and slowly lower the bar down to the thighs. Slightly flex the hips and knees to cushion the impact of the bar on the thighs.

☐ At the completion of the set, slowly flex the hips and knees at the same rate (to keep an erect torso position) to return the bar to the floor in a controlled manner.

☐ Reposition the bar and the body for the next repetition.

Hang Clean

This exercise is similar to the power clean with one primary modification: The initial position of the bar is on the thighs, just above the knees, not on the floor. Fundamentally, the hang clean *is* the power clean exercise starting at the beginning of the transition, or scoop, position. Because the bar is moved a shorter distance, there is less time for the lifter to exert a pulling force on the bar. The initial momentum of the bar at the knees is zero, so more muscular effort (power) is required for lifting a given load than in the power clean. Therefore, the forceful, rapid extension of the hips, knees, and ankles followed by the shrugging of the shoulders and pulling with the arms is critical for performing the hang clean exercise.

Starting Position

☐ Observe the preparatory body position and lifting guidelines (see introduction) to place the body in the correct position to lift the bar off the floor.

☐ Using the same stance, grip, and initial body position as in the power clean, slowly lift the bar along the shins and knees until standing erect with the bar resting on the front of the thighs.

Starting position   **Triple extension with shoulder shrug**

☐ From this standing posture with the arms extended and the elbows pointed out to the sides, lean forward and flex the hips and knees slightly to place the bar just above the knees.

☐ All repetitions begin from this position.

Upward Movement

☐ Begin the exercise with a jumping motion by forcefully extending the hips, knees, and ankles (commonly called the *triple extension*).

☐ Keep the shoulders over the bar and the elbows extended as long as possible. As the lower-body joints fully extend, rapidly shrug the shoulders upward but keep the elbows extended and pointing out to the sides.

☐ At maximal shoulder elevation, flex the elbows and pull the body under the bar. The bar should pass as close to the torso as possible.

☐ Continue to pull with the arms as high and as long as possible. These actions will result in the highest bar position.

☐ This jumping movement with the bar will result in an erect or slightly hyper-extended torso and head, and the feet may come up off the floor.

Highest bar position   **Catch**   **Final standing position**

Catch

☐ After the lower body has fully extended and the bar reaches maximal height, catch the bar by pulling the body under it, rotating the arms and hands around then under the bar. Re-flex the hips and knees to approximately a quarter-squat position.

☐ The feet will recontact the floor in a slightly wider stance in comparison to the starting position.

☐ The final standing position of the hang clean is the same as in the power clean: The bar is on the anterior deltoids and clavicles, and the body is fully erect.

Downward Movement

☐ At the completion of the repetition, rotate the arms back around the bar to "unrack" it from the anterior deltoids and clavicles and slowly lower the bar down to the thighs. Slightly flex the hips and knees to cushion the impact of the bar on the thighs.

☐ If additional repetitions are to be performed, stand fully erect *first* and then follow the guidelines to move the body into the correct starting position. The bar does *not* return to the floor between repetitions.

☐ At the completion of the set, slowly flex the hips and knees at the same rate (to keep an erect torso position) to return the bar to the floor in a controlled manner.

Push Press (and Push Jerk)

This exercise consists of quickly and forcefully pushing the bar from the shoulders to over the head. Although the ascent consists of two phases, the upward movement of the bar occurs in one continuous motion without interruption.

Both the push press and the push jerk exercises involve rapid hip and knee extension that accelerates the bar off the shoulders, followed immediately by movements that position the bar overhead. The technique used for attaining this final bar position varies, however. In the push press, the hip and knee extension thrust is only forceful enough to drive the bar one-third to one-half the distance overhead. From this height, the bar is pressed out (hence the name *push press*) to the overhead position, with the hips and knees remaining fully extended after the thrust. This can be seen in the photo labeled "Catch (push press)." The push jerk involves a more forceful hip and knee thrust so that the bar is actually "thrown" (or *jerked*) upward and caught with extended elbows in the overhead position with the hips and knees slightly flexed. This can be seen in the photo labeled "Catch (push jerk)."

Starting Position

☐ Use the power or hang clean exercise to lift the bar from the floor to the shoulders or remove the bar from a shoulder-height position on a power or squat rack.

☐ Stand erect with the feet hip-width apart and the toes pointed forward or slightly outward.

☐ Once the bar is positioned at the front of the shoulders, check to be sure that the grip on the bar is even, pronated, closed, and about shoulder-width apart.

☐ All repetitions begin from this position.

Dip (Active Preparation for Upward Movement Phase)

☐ Keeping the torso erect and head in a neutral position, flex the hips and knees at a slow to moderate speed to move the bar in a straight path downward. Do not change the position of the arms.

☐ The downward movement is not a full squat, but rather a "dip" to a depth not to exceed a quarter-squat or the catch position of the power clean. Another guideline is a depth that does not exceed 10% of the lifter's body height (i.e., about 6 to 8 inches or 15 to 20 cm).

Upward Movement (Drive)

☐ Immediately upon reaching the lowest position of the dip, reverse the movement by rapidly extending the hips, knees, and ankles to move the bar overhead.

☐ Initially, the bar needs to be held firmly in place on the shoulders to benefit maximally from the upward momentum produced by the jumping movement. But as the lower-body joints reach full extension, shrug the shoulders to begin moving the bar upward off the shoulders. Note that the feet may come off the floor as the shoulders elevate.

☐ The neck must slightly hyperextend to allow the bar to pass by the chin (or else the bar will hit the face).

Catch (for the Push Press)

Because the drive phase of the push press is not forceful enough to move the bar to a fully overhead position, the catch phase is similar to the second half of the shoulder press exercise: The hips and knees are already fully extended after the drive and the shoulders (deltoids) and arms (triceps) press the bar up to an overhead position.

Push Press (and Push Jerk)

Starting position

Dip

☐ Once the bar is overhead, establish the following positions:
- ■ Fully extended elbows
- ■ Erect, tight torso
- ■ Neutral head position
- ■ Flat feet
- ■ Bar slightly behind the head

☐ The feet will recontact the floor in a slightly wider stance in comparison to the starting position.

☐ The body's weight should be balanced over the middle of the feet.

☐ Stand in a fully erect body position to gain control of the bar and achieve balance.

Catch (for the Push Jerk)

The drive phase of the push jerk allows the bar to be caught over the head with fully extended elbows and the hips and knees slightly flexed.

☐ As the bar is caught, the hips and knees should be flexed to about a quarter-squat position. The goal is to reach the lowest squat position at the same moment the bar reaches maximal height.

Drive   Catch (push press)   Catch (push jerk)

☐ The feet will recontact the floor in a slightly wider stance in comparison to the starting position.

☐ The torso should be erect with the head in a neutral position directly under the bar; eyes are focused forward.

☐ The body's weight should be balanced over the middle of the feet.

☐ After gaining control and balance, stand up by extending the hips and knees to a fully erect position (not seen in the photo).

Downward Movement

☐ At the completion of the repetition, lower the bar by gradually reducing the muscular tension of the arms to allow a controlled descent of the bar to the shoulders. The hips and knees are simultaneously flexed to cushion the impact of the bar on the shoulders.

☐ If additional repetitions are to be performed, stand fully erect *first* and then follow the guidelines described for the dip phase. The bar does *not* return to the floor between repetitions.

☐ At the completion of the set, first lower the bar from the shoulders to the thighs, then to the floor (similar to the power clean exercise). The bar can also be placed back on the power or squat rack.

LOWER BODY

Hip and Thigh (Multijoint) Exercises

DVD 1

Name	Description of the concentric action	PREDOMINANT MUSCLES INVOLVED	
		Muscle group or body area	Muscles
🖐 Front squat	Hip extension	Gluteals	Gluteus maximus
		Hamstrings	Semimembranosus Semitendinosus Biceps femoris
	Knee extension	*Quadriceps*	Vastus lateralis Vastus intermedius Vastus medialis Rectus femoris
🖐 Back squat	Hip extension	*Gluteals*	Gluteus maximus
		Hamstrings	Semimembranosus Semitendinosus Biceps femoris
	Knee extension	Quadriceps	Vastus lateralis Vastus intermedius Vastus medialis Rectus femoris
Hack squat (machine)	Same as front and back squat		
Deadlift	Same as front and back squat		
Hip sled (machine)	Same as front and back squat		
Horizontal leg press (machine)	Same as front and back squat		
🖐 Step-up	Same as front and back squat		
🖐 Forward step lunge	Same as front and back squat, but with these additions:		
	Hip flexion	Hip flexors (of the trailing leg)	Rectus femoris Iliopsoas
	Ankle plantar flexion	Calf (of the leading leg)	Soleus Gastrocnemius

🖐 Denotes an exercise that requires a spotter. The muscle groups most emphasized in these exercises are in *bolded italics*.

Front Squat

Starting Position: Lifter

☐ With the bar positioned at approximately armpit height on the supporting pins or ledge of shoulder-high rack stands (or in a power or squat rack), move toward the bar and position the front of the shoulders and the hips and feet directly under the bar.

☐ Grasp the bar using one of the following hand and arm positions:

The most common position is the *clean* or *parallel-arm* grip:

■ Grasp the bar evenly with a closed and pronated grip, slightly wider than shoulder-width apart.

Lowest squat position

Parallel-arm position

Crossed-arm position

Starting positions with parallel-arm position

Downward movement positions

- Rotate the arms around the bar to place the bar on top of the anterior deltoids or clavicles. The backs of the hands should be either slightly on top of *or* just outside of the shoulders, right next to where the bar is resting on the deltoids.
- Raise the elbows to lift the upper arms to parallel with the floor. The wrists should be hyperextended and the elbows fully flexed.

An alternative position is the *crossed-arm* grip:

- Flex the elbows and cross the forearms in front of the chest.
- Move the body to position the bar evenly on the anterior deltoids without touching it with the hands.
- Once in the correct location, place the hands on top of the bar and use pressure from the fingers to keep it in position. Note that this is an open grip; the thumb will not be able to encircle the bar because the shoulders will be in the way.
- Move the arms upward to a position parallel to the floor.

☐ For either grip, keep the elbows lifted up and forward. This contributes greatly to securing the bar on the shoulders.

☐ Signal the spotters for assistance and then extend the hips and knees to lift the bar off the supporting pins or ledge and take a step backward. Be aware of the frame of the rack. If performing the front squat on the inside of a four-pole,

Upward movement positions

Racking the bar

LOWER BODY

boxed type of rack, there may be only about 12 to 18 inches (30 to 46 cm) of space for the backward step. Leave enough room (front to back) so that the bar will not strike the frame during the exercise.

☐ Position the feet between hip- and shoulder-width apart with the toes pointed slightly outward so the knees track directly over the feet.

☐ Stand with an erect torso by positioning the shoulders back, tilting the head slightly back, and protruding the chest up and out to create a flat or slightly arched back.

☐ All repetitions begin from this position.

Starting Position: Two Spotters

☐ Stand erect at opposite ends of the bar with the feet shoulder-width apart and the knees slightly flexed.

☐ Grasp the end of the bar by cupping the hands together with the palms facing upward.

☐ At the lifter's signal, assist with lifting and balancing the bar as it is moved off the supporting pins or ledge.

☐ Move sideways in unison with the lifter as the lifter moves backward.

☐ Release the bar smoothly.

☐ Hold the hands 2 to 3 inches (5 to 8 cm) below the ends of the bar.

☐ Once the lifter is in position, assume a shoulder-width stance with the knees slightly flexed and the torso erect.

Downward Movement: Lifter

☐ Begin the exercise by flexing the hips and knees slowly and under control.

☐ Maintain a flat or slightly arched back and rigid arm position; do not round the upper back or lean forward as the bar is lowered.

☐ Focus the eyes ahead and slightly above horizontal, and tilt the head back slightly.

☐ Keep the body's weight over the middle and heel area of the feet; do not allow the heels to rise off the floor during the descent.

☐ Keep the knees aligned over the feet as they flex; avoid letting the knees move beyond the toes during the descent.

☐ Continue the downward movement phase until *one* of these three events occurs (they determine the maximum range of motion, or the lowest squat position):

    1. The thighs are parallel to the floor (if achievable).

    2. The trunk begins to round or flex forward.

    3. The heels rise off the floor.

☐ Actual squat depth is dependent on lower-body joint flexibility.

☐ Keep the body tight and in control; do not bounce or relax the legs and torso at the bottom of the movement.

Downward Movement: Two Spotters

☐ Keep the cupped hands close to—but not touching—the bar as it descends.

☐ Slightly flex the knees, hips, and torso and keep the back flat when following the bar.

Upward Movement: Lifter

☐ Raise the bar under control by extending the hips and knees.

☐ Maintain a flat or slightly arched back and rigid arm position. As the bar is raised, resist the tendency to lean forward by keeping the head tilted slightly back and the chest held up and out.

☐ Move the bar upward by pushing up through the whole foot with the body's weight evenly distributed between the heels and forefoot to keep the feet in contact with the floor and the hips under the bar. Do not allow the body's weight to shift forward onto the balls of the feet.

☐ Keep the knees aligned over the feet; do not allow them to shift inward or outward as they extend.

☐ Continue raising the bar at an even rate until the hips and knees are fully extended and the standing starting position is achieved.

☐ At the completion of the set, signal the spotters for assistance to rack the bar, but keep a grip on the bar until both ends are secure and motionless on the supporting pins or ledge.

Upward Movement: Two Spotters

☐ Keep the cupped hands close to—but not touching—the bar as it ascends.

☐ Slightly extend the knees, hips, and torso and keep the back flat when following the bar.

☐ At the lifter's signal after the set is completed, move sideways in unison with the lifter back to the rack.

☐ Simultaneously grasp the bar and assist with balancing the bar as it is placed back on the supporting pins or ledge.

☐ Release the bar smoothly.

Back Squat

Starting Position: Lifter

☐ With the bar positioned at approximately armpit height on the supporting pins or ledge of shoulder-high rack stands (or in a power or squat rack), move toward the bar and position the base of the neck (or upper middle back) and the hips and feet directly under the bar.

☐ Grasp the bar using one of the following bar placement positions:

To perform the back squat with a *low bar* placement, do the following:

▪ Place the bar evenly *on top of* the posterior deltoids at the middle of the trapezius.

Lowest squat position

High bar position

Low bar position

Starting positions with high bar position

Downward movement positions

- Grasp the bar evenly with a closed and pronated grip, wider than shoulder-width apart. For most people, the hand placement is very wide to compensate for the lower bar position.

- An alternative grip is an open grip, which may be more comfortable for the wrists. If an open grip is used, be aware that it does not provide as much control of the bar as a closed grip.

To perform the back squat with a *high bar* placement, do the following:

- Place the bar evenly *above* the posterior deltoids at the base of the neck.

- Grasp the bar evenly with a closed and pronated grip, slightly wider than shoulder-width apart.

☐ For either bar placement, raise the elbows to create a shelf with the upper-back and shoulder muscles for the bar to rest on. (A high elbow position also allows the arms to maintain pressure on the bar to prevent it from sliding down the back.)

☐ Signal the spotters for assistance and then extend the hips and knees to lift the bar off the supporting pins or ledge and take a step backward. Be aware of the frame of the rack. If performing the back squat on the inside of a four-pole, boxed type of rack, there may be only about 12 to 18 inches (30 to 46 cm) of space for the backward step. Leave enough room (front to back) so that the bar will not strike the frame during the exercise.

Upward movement positions   **Racking the bar**

☐ Position the feet between hip- and shoulder-width apart with the toes pointed slightly outward so the knees track directly over the feet.

☐ Stand with an erect torso by positioning the shoulders back, tilting the head slightly back, and protruding the chest up and out to create a flat or slightly arched back.

☐ All repetitions begin from this position.

Starting Position: Two Spotters

☐ Stand erect at opposite ends of the bar with the feet shoulder-width apart and the knees slightly flexed.

☐ Grasp the end of the bar by cupping the hands together with the palms facing upward.

☐ At the lifter's signal, assist with lifting and balancing the bar as it is moved off the supporting pins or ledge.

☐ Move sideways in unison with the lifter as the lifter moves backward.

☐ Release the bar smoothly.

☐ Hold the hands 2 to 3 inches (5 to 8 cm) below the ends of the bar.

☐ Once the lifter is in position, assume a shoulder-width stance with the knees slightly flexed and the torso erect.

Downward Movement: Lifter

☐ Begin the exercise by flexing the hips and knees slowly and under control.

☐ Maintain a flat or slightly arched back and high elbow position; do not round the upper back or lean forward as the bar is lowered.

☐ Focus the eyes ahead and slightly above horizontal, and tilt the head back slightly.

☐ Keep the body's weight over the middle and heel area of the feet; do not allow the heels to rise off the floor during the descent.

☐ Keep the knees aligned over the feet as they flex; avoid letting the knees move beyond the toes during the descent.

☐ Continue the downward movement phase until *one* of these three events occurs (they determine the maximum range of motion, or the lowest squat position):

    1. The thighs are parallel to the floor (if achievable).

    2. The trunk begins to round or flex forward.

    3. The heels rise off the floor.

☐ Actual squat depth is dependent on lower-body joint flexibility.

☐ Keep the body tight and in control; do not bounce or relax the legs and torso at the bottom of the movement.

Downward Movement: Two Spotters

☐ Keep the cupped hands close to—but not touching—the bar as it descends.

☐ Slightly flex the knees, hips, and torso and keep the back flat when following the bar.

Upward Movement: Lifter

☐ Raise the bar under control by extending the hips and knees.

☐ Maintain a flat or slightly arched back and high elbow position. As the bar is raised, resist the tendency to lean forward by keeping the head tilted slightly back and the chest up and out.

☐ Move the bar upward by pushing up through the whole foot with the body's weight evenly distributed between the heels and forefoot to keep the feet in contact with the floor and the hips under the bar. Do not allow the body's weight to shift forward onto the balls of the feet.

☐ Keep the knees aligned over the feet; do not allow them to shift inward or outward as they extend.

☐ Continue raising the bar at an even rate until the hips and knees are fully extended and the standing starting position is achieved.

☐ At the completion of the set, signal the spotters for assistance to rack the bar, but keep a grip on the bar until both ends are secure and motionless on the supporting pins or ledge.

Upward Movement: Two Spotters

☐ Keep the cupped hands close to—but not touching—the bar as it ascends.

☐ Slightly extend the knees, hips, and torso and keep the back flat when following the bar.

☐ At the lifter's signal after the set is completed, move sideways in unison with the lifter back to the rack.

☐ Simultaneously grasp the bar and assist with balancing the bar as it is placed back on the supporting pins or ledge.

☐ Release the bar smoothly.

Hack Squat (Machine)

Starting Position

☐ Stand inside the machine and lie back with the head and back pressed evenly against their respective pads (i.e., in the center of the pads, not to the left or right side).

☐ Wedge the shoulders under the shoulder pads attached to the machine.

☐ Place the feet shoulder-width apart and flat on the foot platform with the toes pointed slightly outward. The feet should be near the top edge of the foot platform. Both feet must be positioned in the same manner—the same space should be seen between the left foot and the left side of the foot platform as there is between the right foot and the right side of the foot platform. Also, both feet should have an identical toed-out angle.

☐ Position the thighs and lower legs parallel to each other.

☐ Grasp the handles or the machine frame and simultaneously extend the hips and knees to raise the machine 1 to 2 inches (3 to 5 cm).

☐ Keep the head, shoulders, and back pressed evenly against their respective pads.

☐ Remove the support mechanism. Many varieties exist, but most require one or two handles near the hands or body to be turned inward or moved.

☐ Regrasp the handles or the machine frame to help keep the body firmly in place.

☐ Extend the hips and knees—but do not lock out the knees—to raise the machine to the starting position.

☐ All repetitions begin from this position.

Downward Movement

☐ Begin the exercise by flexing the hips and knees slowly and under control.

☐ Keep the head, shoulders, and back pressed evenly against their respective pads.

☐ Keep the thighs and lower legs parallel to each other; any deviations will place undue stress on the low back and knees. Keep the knees aligned over the feet as they flex; avoid letting the knees move beyond the toes during the descent.

☐ Continue the downward movement phase until *one* of these three events occurs (they determine the maximum range of motion, or the bottom position):

    1. The thighs are parallel to the foot platform (if achievable).

    2. The back loses contact with the pad.

    3. The knees move in front of the toes.

☐ The extent of the range of motion depends on the degree of spinal, hip, knee, and ankle flexibility as well as the machine's design features and adjustment capabilities.

☐ At the bottom of the movement, do not relax the legs and torso and do not bounce the machine to spring it back up for the next repetition.

Upward Movement

☐ Push the machine up and under control by extending the hips and knees. The feet should remain flat on the foot platform.

☐ Keep the head, shoulders, and back pressed evenly against their respective pads.

☐ Keep the thighs and lower legs parallel to each other; do not allow the knees to shift inward or outward as they extend.

☐ Continue pushing the machine up until the knees are fully extended but not forcefully locked.

☐ At the completion of the set, slightly flex the hips and knees, turn or move one or two handles to move the supports back into place, lower the machine until it is resting on the supports, and then step out of the machine.

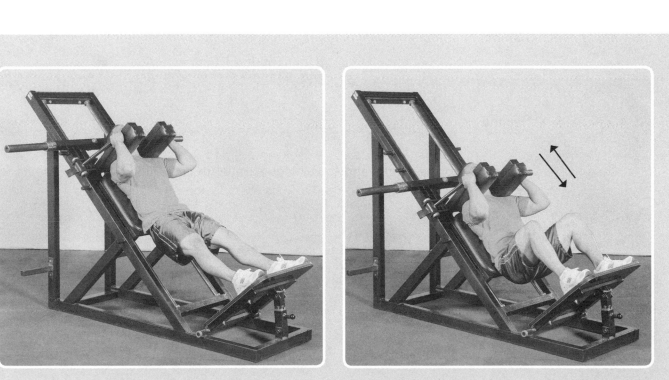

Starting position   **Downward and upward movements**

Deadlift

Starting Position

The initial position for this exercise is identical to that of the power clean except for the hand position. Instead of both hands using a pronated grip, one hand is supinated and the other is pronated. (Typically, the hand that is pronated is the dominant hand.) This hand position is called an *alternated* grip. It is not required to perform the exercise; it simply improves the ability to hold on to the bar with heavier loads. Some people, however, still use a two-hand pronated grip but use wrist straps for an improved grasp on the bar.

☐ Squat down with the hips lower than the shoulders and grasp the bar evenly with an alternated grip shoulder-width (or slightly wider) apart.

☐ Position the feet between hip- and shoulder-width apart with the toes pointed slightly outward so the knees track directly over the feet.

☐ Position the arms outside the knees with the elbows fully extended and pointing out to the sides.

☐ Position the bar approximately 1 inch (3 cm) in front of the shins and over the balls of the feet.

| Starting position | Middle position | End position |

☐ Just before liftoff, observe the preparatory body position and lifting guidelines (see introduction) to place the body in the correct position to lift the bar off the floor. Exact positions of the torso, hips, knees, and bar are related to body segment length and lower-body joint flexibility.

☐ All repetitions begin from this position.

Upward Movement

☐ Begin the exercise by extending the knees and hips slowly and under control. Keep the back or torso angle constant in relation to the floor; do not let the hips rise before or faster than the shoulders, and keep the back flat or slightly arched.

☐ Maintain full elbow extension, with the head neutral in relation to the spine, and the shoulders over or slightly ahead of the bar.

☐ During the ascent, keep the bar as close to the shins as possible and slightly shift the body's weight back toward the heels.

☐ As soon as the bar rises to just above the knees, shift the body's weight forward toward the balls of the feet, keeping the heels on the floor.

☐ Maintain a flat or slightly arched back, with the elbows fully extended and pointing out to the sides, the shoulders over or slightly ahead of the bar, and the head neutral in relation to the spine.

☐ Continue to extend the hips and knees until the body reaches a fully erect or very slightly hyperextended torso position.

Downward Movement

☐ Slowly flex the hips and knees at the same rate to return the bar to the floor in a controlled manner.

☐ During the descent, keep the bar as close to the thighs and shins as possible.

☐ Maintain a flat or slightly arched back, with the elbows fully extended and pointing out to the sides, the shoulders over or slightly ahead of the bar, and the head neutral in relation to the spine.

☐ Touch the plates to the floor, and then immediately (without a pause) lift the bar back up for the next repetition.

Hip Sled (Machine)

Starting Position

☐ Sit inside the machine with the head, back, hips, and buttocks pressed evenly against their respective pads (i.e., in the center of the pads, not to the left or right side). Some machines have shoulder pads that allow the lifter to wedge the shoulders underneath.

☐ All body segments other than the legs must be firmly positioned against their pads to provide maximal support to the spine and low back. If the angle of the back pad is adjustable, move it up or down to allow the torso and legs to form approximately a 90-degree angle (at the hips) when the feet are properly positioned on the foot platform and the knees are fully extended.

☐ Place the feet between hip- and shoulder-width apart and flat on the foot platform with the toes pointed slightly outward. Both feet must be positioned in the same manner—the same space should be seen between the left foot and the left side of the foot platform as there is between the right foot and the right side of the foot platform. Also, both feet should have an identical toed-out angle.

Foot position

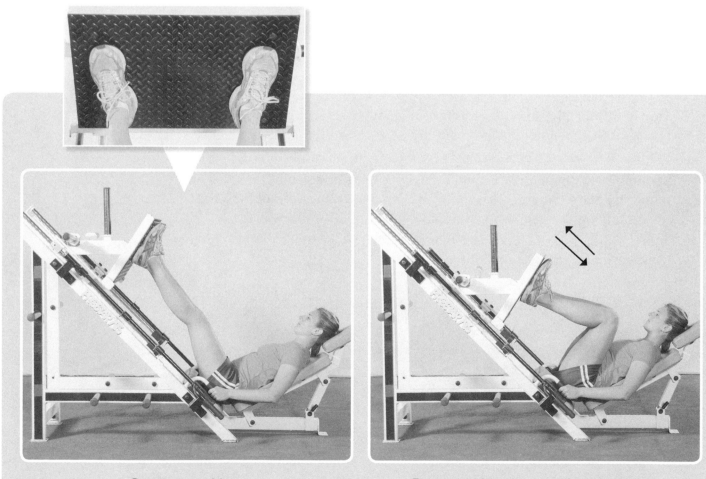

Starting position   **Downward and upward movements**

- ☐ Position the thighs and lower legs parallel to each other.
- ☐ Grasp the handles or the machine frame and simultaneously extend the hips and knees to raise the foot platform 1 to 2 inches (3 to 5 cm).
- ☐ Keep the hips and buttocks on the seat and the back flat against the back pad as the foot platform rises.
- ☐ Remove the support mechanism from the foot platform. Many varieties exist, but most require one or two handles near the body to be turned outward or moved.
- ☐ Regrasp the handles or the machine frame to help keep the body firmly in place.
- ☐ Extend the hips and knees—but do not lock out the knees—to raise the foot platform to the starting position.
- ☐ Maintain a stationary lower body as it braces the foot platform.
- ☐ All repetitions begin from this position.

Downward Movement

- ☐ Begin the exercise by flexing the hips and knees slowly and under control.
- ☐ Keep the hips and buttocks on the seat and the back flat against the back pad.
- ☐ Keep the thighs and lower legs parallel to each other; any deviations will place undue stress on the low back and knees. Keep the knees aligned over the feet as they flex; avoid letting the knees move beyond the toes during the descent.
- ☐ Continue the downward movement phase until *one* of these four events occurs (they determine the maximum range of motion, or the bottom position):
     1. The thighs are parallel to the foot platform (if achievable).
     2. The buttocks lose contact with the seat.
     3. The hips roll off the back pad.
     4. The heels rise off the foot platform.
- ☐ The extent of the range of motion depends on the degree of spinal, hip, knee, and ankle flexibility as well as the machine's design features and adjustment capabilities.
- ☐ At the bottom of the movement, do not relax the legs and torso and do not bounce the foot platform to spring it back up for the next repetition.

Upward Movement

- ☐ Push the foot platform up and under control by extending the hips and knees. The feet should remain flat on the foot platform.
- ☐ Keep the hips and buttocks on the seat and the back flat against the back pad. Do not shift the hips or allow the buttocks to lose contact with the seat.
- ☐ Keep the thighs and lower legs parallel to each other; do not allow the knees to shift inward or outward as they extend.
- ☐ Continue pushing the foot platform up until the knees are fully extended but not forcefully locked.
- ☐ At the completion of the set, slightly flex the hips and knees, turn or move one or two handles to move the supports back into place, lower the foot platform until it is resting on the supports, and then stand up and step out of the machine.

Horizontal Leg Press (Machine)

Starting Position

☐ Lie in the machine with the head, back, hips, and buttocks pressed evenly against their respective pads (i.e., in the center of the pads, not to the left or right side).

☐ Wedge the shoulders under the shoulder pads attached to the machine.

☐ All body segments other than the legs must be firmly positioned against their pads to provide maximal support to the spine and low back. If the horizontal position of the foot platform or the seat is adjustable, move it forward or backward to allow the thighs to be parallel to the foot platform when lying in the starting position.

☐ Place the feet between hip- and shoulder-width apart and flat on the foot platform with the toes pointed slightly outward. Both feet must be positioned in the same manner—the same space should be seen between the left foot and the left side of the foot platform as there is between the right foot and the right side of the foot platform. Also, both feet should have an identical toed-out angle.

☐ Position the thighs and lower legs parallel to each other.

☐ Grasp the handles or the sides of the seat.

☐ All repetitions begin from this position.

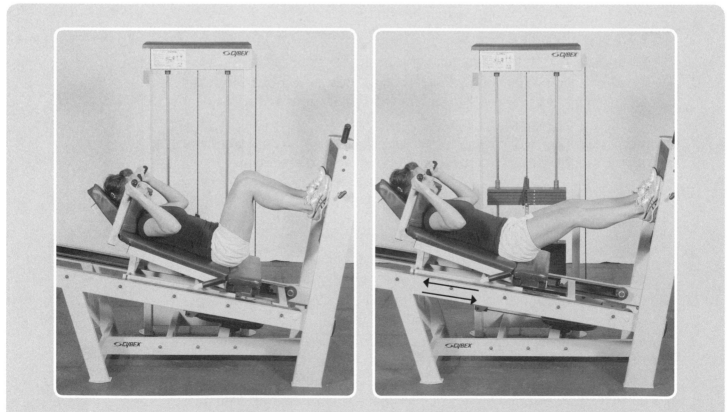

Starting position   **Backward and forward movements**

Backward Movement

☐ Begin the exercise by extending the hips and knees slowly and under control to push the seat *backward*. (Note that in some machines, the seat is fixed and the foot platform will move *forward* during this phase.) The feet should remain flat on the foot platform.

☐ Keep the head, shoulders, back, hips, and buttocks pressed evenly against their respective pads. Do not shift the hips or allow the buttocks to lose contact with the seat.

☐ Keep the thighs and lower legs parallel to each other; do not allow the knees to shift inward or outward as they extend.

☐ Continue the backward movement phase until the knees are fully extended but not forcefully locked.

Forward Movement

☐ Allow the hips and knees to slowly flex to bring the seat back to the starting position.

☐ Keep the head, shoulders, back, hips, and buttocks pressed evenly against their respective pads.

☐ Keep the thighs and lower legs parallel to each other; any deviations will place undue stress on the low back and knees. Keep the knees aligned over the feet as they flex.

☐ Continue flexing the hips and knees until the thighs are parallel to the foot platform.

☐ At the completion of the set, release the handles or the sides of the seat and come out or off of the machine.

Step-Up

The box used for this exercise should have a top surface area that allows the lifter's whole foot (shoe) to fit with extra space behind the heel and ahead of the toe. It should be 12 to 18 inches (30 to 46 cm) high, or high enough to create a 90-degree angle at the knee and hip joints when the lead foot is on the box. Also, the box should be placed on a nonslip floor and have a nonslip top surface. Note: to allow an optimal view of the exercise technique, a power or squat rack is not shown in the photos.

Starting Position: Lifter

☐ With the bar positioned at approximately armpit height on the *outside* of a power or squat rack, move toward the bar and position the base of the neck (or upper middle back) and the hips and feet directly under the bar.

☐ Place the bar evenly above the posterior deltoids at the base of the neck (as seen in the high bar position in the back squat exercise).

☐ Grasp the bar evenly with a closed and pronated grip, slightly wider than shoulder-width apart.

☐ Raise the elbows to create a shelf with the upper-back and shoulder muscles for the bar to rest on. (A high elbow position also allows the arms to maintain pressure on the bar to prevent it from sliding down the back.)

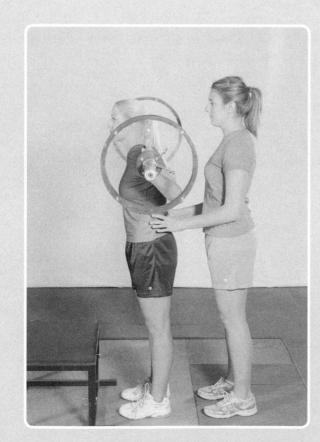

Starting positions

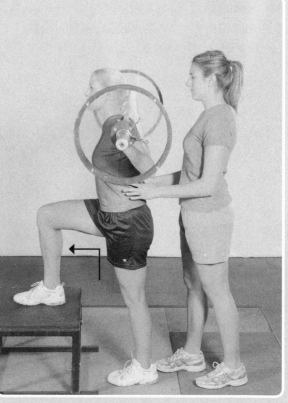

Initial contact of lead foot with top of box

☐ Signal the spotter for assistance and then extend the hips and knees to lift the bar off the supporting pins or ledge. Move to a spot that is the same distance from the box as the height of the box.

☐ Place the feet hip-width apart with the toes pointed ahead.

☐ All repetitions begin from this position.

Starting Position: Spotter

☐ Stand erect and very close behind the lifter (but not so close as to be a distraction).

☐ Place the feet shoulder-width apart with the knees slightly flexed.

☐ At the lifter's signal, assist with lifting and balancing the bar as it is moved out of the rack.

☐ Move in unison with the lifter as the lifter moves to the starting position.

☐ Once the lifter is in position, assume a hip-width stance with the knees slightly flexed and the torso erect.

☐ Position the hands near the lifter's hips, waist, or torso.

Upward Movement: Lifter

☐ Begin the exercise by stepping up with one leg (the lead leg). The initial contact of the lead foot with the top of the box must be made by the entire foot; do not allow the heel to hang off the edge of the box.

Beginning of upward movement positions   **Completion of upward movement positions**

☐ Keep the torso erect; do not lean forward.

☐ Keep the trailing foot in the starting position, but shift the body weight to the lead leg.

☐ Forcefully extend the lead hip and knee to move the body up and on top of the box; do not push off or hop up with the trailing leg or foot.

☐ Keep the torso erect; do not lean forward. As the hip and knee of the lead leg fully extend to a standing position on top of the box, bring the trailing foot up and place it next to the lead foot.

☐ At the highest position, stand erect and pause before beginning the downward movement phase.

Upward Movement: Spotter

☐ Take a small step forward with the lead leg as the lifter steps up on the box.

☐ As the lifter reaches the highest position, bring the trailing leg forward to be next to the lead leg.

☐ Keep the hands as near as possible to the lifter's hips, waist, or torso.

☐ Assist only when necessary to keep the lifter balanced.

Downward Movement: Lifter

☐ Shift the body weight to the same lead leg.

☐ Step off the box with the same trailing leg.

☐ Maintain an erect torso position.

☐ Place the trailing foot on the floor 12 to 18 inches (30 to 46 cm) away from the box.

☐ When the trailing foot is in full contact with the floor, shift the body weight to the trailing leg.

☐ Step off the box with the lead leg.

☐ Bring the lead foot back to a position next to the trailing foot.

☐ Stand erect in the starting position, pause to gain full balance, then alternate lead legs and repeat the movement with the new lead leg. (Some lifters may benefit from repeating the action words "up-up-down-down" during the set to help perform the exercise correctly.)

☐ At the completion of the set, signal the spotter for assistance to rack the bar but keep a grip on the bar until both ends are secure and motionless on the supporting pins or ledge.

Downward Movement: Spotter

☐ Take a small step backward with the same trailing leg as the lifter steps back down to the floor.

☐ As the lifter steps off the box with the lead leg, take a step backward with the same lead leg.

☐ Keep the hands near the lifter's hips, waist, or torso.

☐ Stand erect in the starting position, pause to wait for the lifter, and alternate lead legs.

☐ Assist only when necessary to keep the lifter balanced.

☐ At the lifter's signal after the set is completed, help the lifter rack the bar.

Forward Step Lunge

This exercise can be performed in a variety of ways in many directions. For many people, performing this exercise with only the body as the weight is enough. Well-trained lifters can use a bar (as explained in the following section) for additional resistance. An alternative is to hold a pair of dumbbells at the sides; this is especially helpful if balancing a bar across the shoulders is too difficult or if an experienced spotter is not available. In any situation, a large (or at least long) floor space is required for this exercise. Note: to allow an optimal view of the exercise technique, a power or squat rack is not shown in the photos.

Starting Position: Lifter

☐ With the bar positioned at approximately armpit height on the *outside* of a power or squat rack, move toward the bar and position the base of the neck (or upper middle back) and the hips and feet directly under the bar.

☐ Place the bar evenly above the posterior deltoids at the base of the neck (as seen in the high bar position in the back squat exercise).

☐ Grasp the bar evenly with a closed and pronated grip, slightly wider than shoulder-width apart.

☐ Raise the elbows to create a shelf with the upper-back and shoulder muscles for the bar to rest on. (A high elbow position also allows the arms to maintain pressure on the bar to prevent it from sliding down the back.)

☐ Signal the spotter for assistance, then extend the hips and knees to lift the bar off the supporting pins or ledge. Take two or three steps backward.

☐ Place the feet hip-width apart with the toes pointed ahead.

☐ All repetitions begin from this position.

Starting Position: Spotter

☐ Stand erect and very close behind the lifter (but not close enough to be a distraction).

☐ Place the feet shoulder-width apart with the knees slightly flexed.

☐ At the lifter's signal, assist with lifting and balancing the bar as it is moved out of the rack.

☐ Move in unison with the lifter as the lifter moves backward to the starting position.

☐ Once the lifter is in position, assume a hip-width stance with the knees slightly flexed and the torso erect.

☐ Position the hands near the lifter's hips, waist, or torso.

Forward Movement: Lifter

☐ Begin the exercise by taking one exaggerated step directly forward with one leg; this leg is called the lead leg.

☐ Keep the torso erect and arms tight as the lead foot moves forward and contacts the floor. The trailing foot remains in its starting position, but as the lead leg steps forward, balance shifts to the ball of the trailing foot and the trailing knee flexes slightly.

☐ Plant the lead foot flat on the floor with the toes pointing ahead or slightly inward. To help maintain balance, this foot needs to be placed directly ahead from its initial position and the lead ankle, knee, and hip must be in one vertical plane. Do not step slightly to the right or left or allow the knee to shift in or out.

☐ Once balance has shifted to both feet and stability is achieved, flex the lead knee to lower the trailing knee toward the floor. The trailing knee will flex somewhat farther, but not to the same degree as the lead knee.

☐ The torso must stay erect with the shoulders held back and the head facing forward. Sit back on the trailing leg; do not lean forward or look down.

☐ The lowest ideal body position is with the trailing knee 1 to 2 inches (3 to 5 cm) away from the floor, the lead knee flexed to about 90 degrees, the lead lower leg perpendicular to the floor, and the lead foot flat on the floor. The lead knee must not extend past the toes of the lead foot. Actual lunge depth depends primarily on hip joint flexibility, especially in the iliopsoas muscles.

☐ Allow the ankle of the trailing foot to fully dorsiflex with the toes fully extended.

Forward Step Lunge

Starting positions　　　　**Beginning of forward movement positions**

Forward Movement: Spotter

☐ Step forward with the same lead leg as the lifter.

☐ Keep the lead knee and foot aligned with the lifter's lead knee and foot.

☐ Plant the lead foot 12 to 18 inches (30 to 46 cm) behind the lifter's lead foot.

☐ Flex the lead knee as the lifter's lead knee flexes.

☐ Keep the torso erect.

☐ Keep the hands near the lifter's hips, waist, or torso.

☐ Assist only when necessary to keep the lifter balanced.

Backward Movement: Lifter

☐ Shift the balance forward to the lead foot and forcefully push off the floor with the lead foot by plantar-flexing the ankle of the lead foot and by extending the lead knee and hip joints. Do not jerk the upper body back; maintain its vertical position.

☐ As the lead foot moves back toward the trailing foot, balance will shift back to the trailing foot. This will cause the heel of the trailing foot to regain contact with the floor.

☐ Carry the lead foot back to place it next to the trailing foot. Do not stutter-step backward.

Completion of forward movement positions   **Backward movement positions**

☐ As the lead foot is placed flat on the floor in its starting position, evenly divide the body's weight over both feet. The torso should be erect, similar to the starting position.

☐ Stand erect in the starting position, pause to gain full balance, then alternate lead legs and repeat the movement with the new lead leg.

☐ Some lifters may benefit from mentally dividing the movement into smaller portions during the set to help perform the exercise correctly:

    1. Step forward.

    2. Plant the lead foot.

    3. Lunge down and back.

    4. Stand up.

    5. Push off.

☐ At the completion of the set, signal the spotter for assistance to rack the bar, but keep a grip on the bar until both ends are secure and motionless on the supporting pins or ledge.

Backward Movement: Spotter

☐ Push backward with the lead leg in unison with the lifter.

☐ Bring the lead foot back to a position next to the trailing foot; do not stutter-step backward.

☐ Keep the hands near the lifter's hips, waist, or torso.

☐ Stand erect in the starting position, pause to wait for the lifter, and alternate lead legs.

☐ Assist only when necessary to keep the lifter balanced.

☐ At the lifter's signal after the set is completed, help the lifter rack the bar.

Hip and Thigh (Single-Joint) Exercises

Name	Description of the concentric action	PREDOMINANT MUSCLES INVOLVED	
		Muscle group or body area	Muscles
Stiff-leg deadlift	Hip extension	Gluteals	Gluteus maximus
		Hamstrings	Semimembranosus Semitendinosus Biceps femoris
	Spinal extension	Spinal erectors*	Erector spinae
Good morning	Hip extension	Hamstrings	Semimembranosus Semitendinosus Biceps femoris
		Gluteals	Gluteus maximus
	Spinal extension	Spinal erectors*	Erector spinae
Leg (knee) extension (machine)	Knee extension	Quadriceps	Vastus lateralis Vastus intermedius Vastus medialis Rectus femoris
Lying leg (knee) curl (machine)	Knee flexion	Hamstrings	Semimembranosus Semitendinosus Biceps femoris
Seated leg (knee) curl (machine)	Same as lying leg (knee) curl (machine)		

*Many references consider the spinal erectors stabilizers for these two exercises.

Stiff-Leg Deadlift

Very well-trained lifters may stand on a raised platform to perform this exercise through a greater range of motion. Instead of touching the plates to the floor, the lifter can lower the bar to touch the feet. Note that this requires an extremely large degree of flexibility in the hamstrings, gluteals, and low back; therefore most people should not use a raised platform. Nearly all lifters should stand on the floor and safely lower the bar only to knee or middle-shin level.

Starting Position

☐ Observe the preparatory body position and lifting guidelines (see introduction) to place the body in the correct position to lift the bar off the floor.

☐ Perform the starting position and upward movement phases of the deadlift exercise.

☐ The bar and body position achieved at the end of the upward movement phase of the deadlift exercise is the starting position for the stiff-leg deadlift exercise, but with one important exception: The knees are slightly to moderately flexed and *remain in this position* throughout the downward and upward movement phases of the stiff-leg deadlift exercise.

☐ All repetitions begin from this position.

Starting position   **Downward and upward movements**

Downward Movement

☐ Begin the exercise by forming a flat or slightly arched back, and then flex forward at the hips slowly and under control.

☐ During the descent, keep the knees in the same slightly or moderately flexed position with the back flat or slightly arched and the elbows fully extended.

☐ Continue the downward movement phase until *one* of these four events occurs (they determine the maximum range of motion, or the bottom position):

    1. The plates touch the floor (or the bar touches the feet of well-trained lifters standing on a raised platform).

    2. The back cannot be held in the flat or slightly arched position.

    3. The knees fully extend.

    4. The heels rise off the floor.

☐ Keep the body tight and in control; do not bounce or relax the torso at the bottom of the movement.

Upward Movement

☐ Raise the bar by extending the hips.

☐ During the ascent, keep the knees in the same slightly or moderately flexed position with the back flat or slightly arched and the elbows fully extended.

☐ Continue the upward movement phase until the standing starting position is achieved.

☐ At the completion of the set, slowly flex the hips and knees at the same rate (to keep an erect torso position) to squat down and return the bar to the floor in a controlled manner.

Good Morning

Starting Position

Note: to allow an optimal view of the exercise technique, a power or squat rack is not shown in the photos.

☐ With the bar positioned at approximately armpit height on the *outside* of a power or squat rack, move toward the bar and position the base of the neck (or upper middle back) and the hips and feet directly under the bar.

☐ Place the bar evenly above the posterior deltoids at the base of the neck (as seen in the high bar position in the back squat exercise).

☐ Grasp the bar evenly with a closed and pronated grip, slightly wider than shoulder-width apart.

☐ Raise the elbows to create a shelf with the upper-back and shoulder muscles for the bar to rest on. (A high elbow position also allows the arms to maintain pressure on the bar to prevent it from sliding down the back.)

☐ To remove the bar from the rack, extend the hips and knees to lift the bar off the supporting pins or ledge and take a few steps backward. (Be aware of any space limitations around the power or squat rack.)

☐ Position the body with the
   ■ feet between hip- and shoulder-width apart;
   ■ knees slightly flexed;
   ■ toes angled slightly outward (about 10 degrees);
   ■ torso erect with shoulders back, head tilted slightly back, chest up and out to create a flat or slightly arched back; and
   ■ elbows held up to keep the bar in position.

☐ All repetitions begin from this position.

Downward Movement

☐ Begin the exercise by flexing the hips slowly and under control. The buttocks should move straight back during the descent and the knees should remain slightly flexed.

☐ Maintain a flat or slightly arched back and high elbow position. Focus the eyes ahead and slightly above horizontal, and tilt the head back slightly.

☐ The bar should be slightly behind the toes as it descends; do not allow the heels to rise off the floor.

☐ Continue the downward movement phase until the torso is parallel to the floor. If unable to achieve the parallel position, continue the exercise only as far as proper technique is maintained.

☐ Keep the body tight and in control; do not bounce or relax the torso at the bottom of the movement.

Upward Movement

☐ Raise the bar by extending the hips slowly and under control; keep the knees slightly flexed.

☐ Maintain a flat or slightly arched back and high elbow position with the head tilted back.

☐ Continue the upward movement phase until the standing starting position is achieved.

☐ At the completion of the set, slowly walk forward and return the bar to the supporting pins or ledge.

Starting position   **Downward and upward movements**

Leg (Knee) Extension (Machine)

Starting Position

☐ Sit erect on the seat with the back and hips pressed evenly against their respective pads (i.e., in the center of the pads, not to the left or right side).

☐ Hook the feet under the roller pad; if it is adjustable, position the pad to be in contact with the insteps of the feet (while in the seated position). This might require someone else to reposition the roller pad, or it might require a trial-and-error approach of sitting in the machine, checking the roller pad, getting out and making adjustments, sitting back down, and rechecking it.

☐ The position in the machine must allow the knees to be in line with the axis of rotation of the machine. If the back pad is adjustable, move it forward or backward to create this alignment.

☐ Position the thighs, lower legs, and feet hip-width apart and parallel to each other.

☐ Grasp the side handles or seat pad.

☐ All repetitions begin from this position.

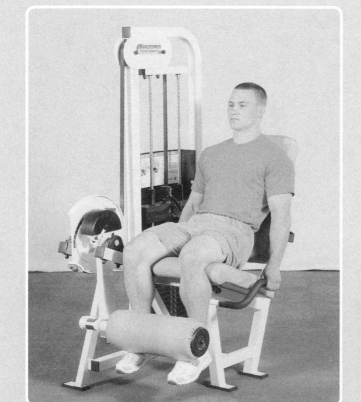

Starting position

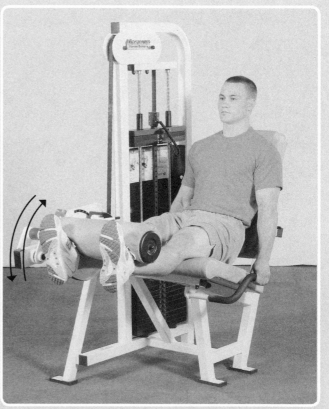

Upward and downward movements

Upward Movement

☐ Begin the exercise by extending the knees slowly and under control.

☐ Keep the thighs, lower legs, and feet parallel to each other; do not allow the thighs to shift inward or outward (i.e., medially or laterally rotate at the hip) as the knees extend.

☐ Keep a tight grasp on the handles or seat pad during the ascent to minimize upper-body and thigh movement.

☐ Do not swing the legs or jerk the torso backward to help raise the weight.

☐ Continue the upward movement phase until the knees are fully extended but not forcefully locked.

Downward Movement

☐ Allow the knees to flex to lower the roller pad slowly and under control back to the starting position.

☐ Do not lower the weight stack uncontrollably.

☐ Keep the thighs, lower legs, and feet parallel to each other.

☐ The back and hips should remain in contact with their respective pads.

☐ At the completion of the set, unhook the feet from under the roller pad and step out of the machine.

Lying Leg (Knee) Curl (Machine)

Starting Position

☐ Lie prone on the bench with the torso, hips, and thighs resting evenly on their respective pads (i.e., in the center of the pads, not to the left or right side).

☐ Hook the feet under the roller pad; if it is adjustable, position the pad to be in contact with the back of the heels, just above the top of the shoes (when lying prone). This might require someone else to reposition the roller pad, or it might require a trial-and-error approach of lying in the machine, checking the roller pad, getting out and making adjustments, lying back down, and rechecking it.

☐ The position in the machine must allow the knees to be in line with the axis of rotation of the machine. This typically requires the knees (i.e., at least the patella) to hang off the end of the thigh pad.

☐ Position the thighs, lower legs, and feet hip-width apart and parallel to each other.

☐ Grasp the handles or torso pad.

☐ All repetitions begin from this position.

Starting position

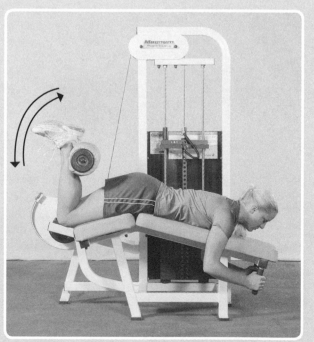

Upward and downward movements

Upward Movement

☐ Begin the exercise by flexing the knees slowly and under control.

☐ Keep the thighs, lower legs, and feet parallel to each other; do not allow the thighs to shift inward or outward (i.e., medially or laterally rotate at the hip) as the knees flex.

☐ Keep a tight grasp on the handles or torso pad during the ascent to minimize upper-body and thigh movement.

☐ To reduce the stress on the low back, do not allow the hips to rise (via hip flexion); this is especially important when using flat-bench leg (knee) curl machines.

☐ Do not move the upper body or kick back with the legs to help raise the weight.

☐ Continue the upward movement phase until the roller pad nearly touches the buttocks. Actual range of motion will depend on the length of the limbs, the flexibility of the quadriceps, and the design of the machine.

Downward Movement

☐ Allow the knees to extend to lower the roller pad slowly and under control back to the starting position.

☐ Do not lower the weight stack uncontrollably.

☐ Keep the thighs, lower legs, and feet parallel to each other.

☐ The torso, hips, and thighs should remain in contact with their respective pads.

☐ At the completion of the set, unhook the feet from under the roller pad and step out of the machine.

Seated Leg (Knee) Curl (Machine)

Starting Position

☐ Raise the thigh pad to its highest position.

☐ Sit erect on the seat with the back and hips pressed evenly against their respective pads (i.e., in the center of the pads, not to the left or right side).

☐ Extend the knees and place the feet on top of the roller pad; if it is adjustable, position the pad to be in contact with the back of the heels or lower calves, just above the top of the shoes (when seated). This might require someone else to reposition the roller pad, or it might require a trial-and-error approach of sitting in the machine, checking the roller pad, getting out and making adjustments, sitting back down, and rechecking it.

☐ The position in the machine must allow the knees to be in line with the axis of rotation of the machine. If the back pad is adjustable, move it forward or backward to create this alignment.

☐ Position the thighs, lower legs, and feet hip-width apart and parallel to each other.

☐ Lower the thigh pad so it *firmly* presses against the thighs.

☐ Grasp the side handles or seat pad.

☐ All repetitions begin from this position.

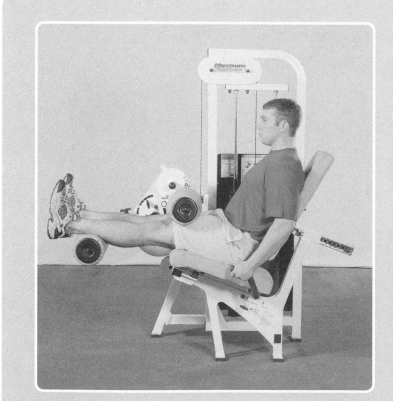

Starting position

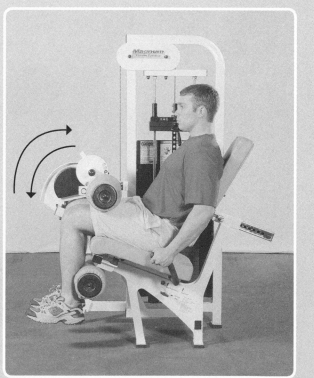

Downward and upward movements

Downward Movement

☐ Begin the exercise by flexing the knees slowly and under control.

☐ Keep the thighs, lower legs, and feet parallel to each other; do not allow the thighs to shift inward or outward (i.e., medially or laterally rotate at the hip) as the knees flex.

☐ Keep a tight grasp on the handles or seat pad to minimize upper-body and thigh movement.

☐ Do not move the upper body or kick back with the legs to help raise the weight.

☐ Continue the downward movement phase until the knees are flexed at least 90 degrees. Actual range of motion will depend on the length of the limbs, the flexibility of the quadriceps, and the design of the machine.

Upward Movement

☐ Allow the knees to extend to raise the roller pad slowly and under control back to the starting position.

☐ Do not lower the weight stack uncontrollably.

☐ Keep the thighs, lower legs, and feet parallel to each other.

☐ The back, hips, and thighs should remain in contact with their respective pads.

☐ At the completion of the set, raise the thigh pad to the highest position, move the heels off the roller pad, and step out of the machine.

Calf (Single-Joint) Exercises

DVD 1

Name	Description of the concentric action	PREDOMINANT MUSCLES INVOLVED	
		Muscle group or body area	Muscles
Seated calf (heel) raise (machine)	Ankle plantar flexion	Calf	***Soleus*** Gastrocnemius
Standing calf (heel) raise (machine)	Same as seated calf (heel) raise (machine)		Soleus ***Gastrocnemius***

The portion of the calf most emphasized in these exercises is in ***bolded italics***.

Seated Calf (Heel) Raise (Machine)

Starting Position

☐ Raise the thigh (knee) pad to its highest position.

☐ Sit erect on the seat and place the balls of the feet (metatarsals) on the nearest edge of the step with the legs and feet hip-width apart and parallel to each other.

☐ If the seat height is adjustable, position it to place the thighs parallel to the floor (when the feet are in position).

☐ Lower the thigh (knee) pad so it *firmly* presses against the knees and front of the lower-thigh area (actual contact of the pad depends on the length of the thighs, seat height, and design of the machine).

☐ Grasp the handles.

☐ Plantar-flex the ankles to raise the thigh (knee) pad 1 to 2 inches (3 to 5 cm).

☐ Remove the support mechanism. Many varieties exist, but most require a handle near the hands or body to be turned outward or moved.

☐ Slowly allow the heels to lower fully under control to a comfortable, stretched position.

☐ All repetitions begin from this position.

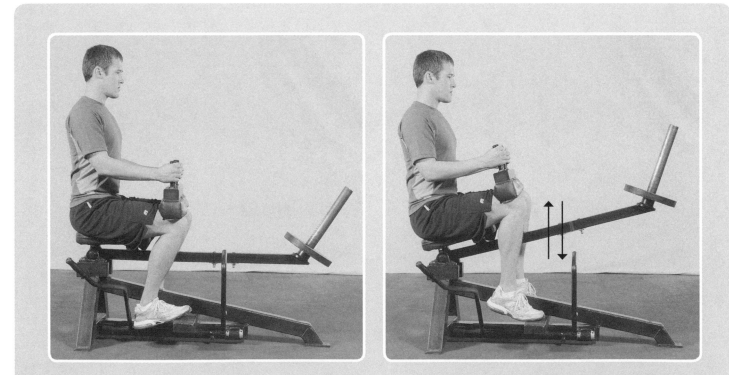

Starting position   **Upward and downward movements**

Upward Movement

☐ Begin the exercise by plantar-flexing the ankles slowly and under control.

☐ Keep the torso erect and the legs and feet parallel to each other.

☐ Apply even pressure on all of the metatarsals; do not slightly invert or evert the feet to rise up only on the big or little toes.

☐ Do not use the arms to pull on the handles or thigh (knee) pad to help raise the weight.

☐ Continue the upward movement phase until the calf muscles are fully contracted (i.e., the ankles are fully plantar flexed).

Downward Movement

☐ Allow the heels to lower slowly and under control back to the starting position.

☐ At the bottom of the movement, do not bounce the weight to spring it back up for the next repetition.

☐ At the completion of the set, slightly plantar-flex the ankles, turn or move the handle to move the support back into place, and then stand up and step out of the machine.

Standing Calf (Heel) Raise (Machine)

Starting Position

☐ Position the body evenly under the shoulder pads and stand erect. The hips should be under the shoulders with the knees fully extended but not forcefully locked.

☐ Grasp the handles.

☐ Place the balls of the feet (metatarsals) on the nearest edge of the step with the legs and feet hip-width apart and parallel to each other. Reposition the body so the hips are under the shoulders and the knees are fully extended but not forcefully locked.

☐ Slowly allow the heels to lower fully under control to a comfortable, stretched position. (The weight to be lifted should be *above* its resting position when the heels are in their lowest stretched position. If not, lower the height of the shoulder pads 2 to 3 inches [5 to 8 cm].)

☐ All repetitions begin from this position.

Starting position   **Upward and downward movements**

Upward Movement

☐ Begin the exercise by plantar-flexing the ankles slowly and under control.

☐ Keep the torso erect and the legs and feet parallel to each other.

☐ Apply even pressure on all of the metatarsals; do not slightly invert or evert the feet to rise up only on the big or little toes.

☐ Do not push or swing the hips forward to help raise the weight.

☐ Continue the upward movement phase until the calf muscles are fully contracted (i.e., the ankles are fully plantar flexed).

Downward Movement

☐ Allow the heels to lower slowly and under control back to the starting position.

☐ At the bottom of the movement, do not bounce the weight to spring it back up for the next repetition.

☐ At the completion of the set, slowly flex the hips and knees to lower the weight to its resting position and then step out of the machine.

LOWER BODY

UPPER BODY

Chest (Multijoint) Exercises

DVD 2

Name	Description of the concentric action	PREDOMINANT MUSCLES INVOLVED	
		Muscle group or body area	Muscles
🖐 Flat barbell bench press	Shoulder transverse (horizontal) adduction	Chest	Pectoralis major
		Shoulders	Anterior deltoid
	Scapular protraction (abduction)	Scapulae	Serratus anterior
		Chest	Pectoralis minor
	Elbow extension	Upper arm (posterior)	Triceps brachii
🖐 Incline barbell bench press	Same as flat barbell bench press		
🖐 Flat dumbell bench press	Same as flat barbell bench press		
🖐 Incline dumbbell bench press	Same as flat barbell bench press		
Flat bench press (Smith machine)	Same as flat barbell bench press		
Vertical chest press (machine)	Same as flat barbell bench press		
Assisted dip (machine)	Shoulder flexion	Chest	Pectoralis major
		Shoulders	Anterior deltoid
	Elbow extension	Upper arm (posterior)	Triceps brachii

🖐 Denotes an exercise that requires a spotter.

Flat Barbell Bench Press

Starting Position: Lifter

☐ Lie supine on a flat bench and position the body to achieve a five-point body-contact position:

    1. Head is placed firmly on the bench.

    2. Shoulders and upper back are placed firmly and evenly on the bench.

    3. Buttocks are placed evenly on the bench.

    4. Right foot is flat on the floor.

    5. Left foot is flat on the floor.

☐ Adjust the body on the bench to position the eyes directly below the racked bar.

☐ Grasp the bar evenly with a closed and pronated grip, slightly wider than shoulder-width apart.

☐ Signal the spotter for assistance to move the bar off the racks to a position over the chest with the elbows fully extended. This is the liftoff. All repetitions begin from this position.

Starting Position: Spotter

☐ Stand erect behind the head of the bench.

☐ Place the feet shoulder-width apart with the knees slightly flexed.

        Liftoff   **Starting positions**

☐ Grasp the bar with a closed and alternated grip inside the lifter's hands.

☐ At the lifter's signal, assist with moving the bar off the racks.

☐ Guide the bar to a position over the lifter's chest.

☐ Release the bar smoothly.

Downward Movement: Lifter

☐ Begin the exercise by lowering the bar slowly and under control toward the chest.

☐ The elbows move down past the torso and slightly away from the body.

☐ Keep the wrists stiff and the forearms perpendicular to the floor and parallel to each other. The width of the grip will determine how parallel the forearms are to each other.

☐ Lower the bar to lightly touch the chest at approximately nipple level; do not bounce the bar on the chest or arch the low back to raise the chest to meet the bar.

☐ Keep the head, torso, hips, and feet in a five-point body-contact position.

Downward Movement: Spotter

☐ Keep the hands in the alternated grip position close to—but not touching—the bar as it descends.

☐ Slightly flex the knees, hips, and torso and keep the back flat when following the bar.

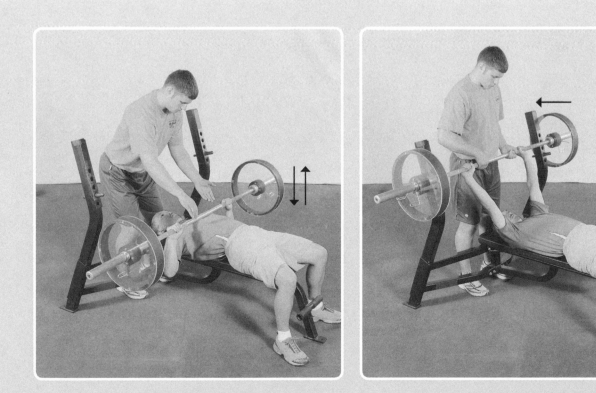

Downward and upward movements   **Racking the bar**

Upward Movement: Lifter

☐ Press the bar up and very slightly backward.

☐ Maintain the same stationary five-point body-contact position; do not arch the low back or lift the buttocks or feet.

☐ Keep the wrists stiff and the forearms perpendicular to the floor and parallel to each other.

☐ Continue pressing the bar up until the elbows are fully extended but not forcefully locked.

☐ At the completion of the set, signal the spotter for assistance to rack the bar, but keep a grip on the bar until both ends are secure and motionless on the supporting pins or ledge.

Upward Movement: Spotter

☐ Keep the hands in the alternated grip position close to—but not touching—the bar as it ascends.

☐ Slightly extend the knees, hips, and torso and keep the back flat when following the bar.

☐ At the lifter's signal after the set is completed, grasp the bar with an alternated grip inside the lifter's hands.

☐ Guide the bar back onto the rack.

☐ Keep a grip on the bar until it is secure and motionless on the supporting pins or ledge.

Incline Barbell Bench Press

Starting Position: Lifter

☐ Before performing this exercise, check the height of the seat and adjust it to allow for the following conditions:

- ■ The thighs are approximately parallel to the floor (with the feet flat). The head is lower than the racked bar and resting at the top of the bench.
- ■ The bar can be lifted off and returned to the supporting pins or ledge without hitting the top of the head (the seat is too high) or requiring the use of the legs to help reach the racks (the seat is too low).

☐ Sit on the seat of an incline bench and then lean back to place the body in a five-point body-contact position:

1. Head is placed firmly against the bench.
2. Shoulders and upper back are placed firmly and evenly against the bench.
3. Buttocks are placed evenly on the seat.
4. Right foot is flat on the floor.
5. Left foot is flat on the floor.

☐ Grasp the bar evenly with a closed and pronated grip, slightly wider than shoulder-width apart.

☐ Signal the spotter for assistance to move the bar off the racks to a position over the neck and face with the elbows fully extended. This is the liftoff. All repetitions begin from this position.

Starting Position: Spotter

☐ Stand erect behind the head of the bench.

☐ Place the feet shoulder-width apart with the knees slightly flexed.

☐ Grasp the bar with a closed and alternated grip inside the lifter's hands.

☐ At the lifter's signal, assist with moving the bar off the racks.

☐ Guide the bar to a position over the lifter's neck and face.

☐ Release the bar smoothly.

Downward Movement: Lifter

☐ Begin the exercise by lowering the bar slowly and under control. It will have a tendency to move away from the body, depending on the angle of the bench, but guide it toward the upper-chest area.

☐ The elbows move down past the torso and slightly away from the body.

☐ Keep the wrists stiff and the forearms perpendicular to the floor and parallel to each other. The width of the grip will determine how parallel the forearms are to each other.

☐ Lower the bar to lightly touch the chest at approximately the upper one-third area of the chest, between the clavicles and the nipples; do not bounce the bar on the chest or arch the low back to raise the chest to meet the bar.

☐ Keep the head, torso, hips, and feet in a five-point body-contact position.

Downward Movement: Spotter

☐ Keep the hands in the alternated grip position close to—but not touching—the bar as it descends.

☐ Slightly flex the knees, hips, and torso and keep the back flat when following the bar.

Upward Movement: Lifter

☐ Press the bar upward and very slightly backward. To keep it from falling forward (because of the angled torso position), press the bar up so it passes close by the face as opposed to out away from the chest.

☐ Do not arch the low back, raise the hips, or push up with the legs (by trying to stand up); the body and feet should not move from their initial positions.

☐ Keep the wrists stiff and the forearms perpendicular to the floor and parallel to each other.

☐ Continue pressing the bar up until the elbows are fully extended but not forcefully locked.

Incline Barbell Bench Press

Starting positions

Downward and upward movements

☐ At the completion of the set, signal the spotter for assistance to rack the bar, but keep a grip on the bar until both ends are secure and motionless on the supporting pins or ledge.

Upward Movement: Spotter

☐ Keep the hands in the alternated grip position close to—but not touching—the bar as it ascends.

☐ Slightly extend the knees, hips, and torso and keep the back flat when following the bar.

☐ At the lifter's signal after the set is completed, grasp the bar with an alternated grip inside the lifter's hands.

☐ Guide the bar back onto the rack.

☐ Keep a grip on the bar until it is secure and motionless on the supporting pins or ledge.

Flat Dumbbell Bench Press

Starting Position: Lifter

☐ Grasp two equal-weight dumbbells with a closed grip. Position the outside surface of the little-finger half of the dumbbells against the front of the thighs (the dumbbell handles will be parallel to each other).

☐ Sit on one end of a flat bench with the dumbbells resting on the thighs.

☐ Lie back so the head rests on the other end of the bench. As the supine position is achieved, first move the dumbbells to the chest (armpit) area and then signal the spotter for assistance to move them to an extended-elbow position above the chest with the forearms parallel to each other.

☐ Reposition the head, shoulders, buttocks, and feet to achieve a five-point body-contact position:

    1. Head is placed firmly on the bench.

    2. Shoulders and upper back are placed firmly and evenly on the bench.

    3. Buttocks are placed evenly on the bench.

    4. Right foot is flat on the floor.

    5. Left foot is flat on the floor.

Starting positions

Downward and upward movements

☐ The most common dumbbell position is with the dumbbell handles in line with each other with the palms facing out. Another option is to hold the dumbbells in a neutral position (i.e., parallel to each other with the palms facing each other).

☐ All repetitions begin from this extended-elbow position with the dumbbells supported over the chest.

Starting Position: Spotter

☐ Get into a low (but still erect) body position very close to the head of the bench.

☐ To create a stable spotting position, get into a fully lunged position with one knee on the floor and the foot of the other leg ahead of the rear knee and flat on the floor.

☐ Grasp the lifter's wrists.

☐ At the lifter's signal, assist with moving the dumbbells to a position over the lifter's chest.

☐ Release the lifter's wrists smoothly.

Starting position
(without spotter shown)

Downward and upward movements
(without spotter shown)

Downward Movement: Lifter

☐ Begin the exercise by lowering the dumbbells slowly and under control toward the chest. To maintain a stable body position on the bench, lower the dumbbells at the same rate.

☐ Keep the wrists stiff, the forearms perpendicular to the floor, and the dumbbell handles in line with each other. Minimize all forward-to-backward and side-to-side movement.

☐ Guide the dumbbells down and slightly out to the lateral side of the chest, near the armpits and in the same vertical plane as the nipples.

☐ Usually, the lowest position of the dumbbells is a depth similar to that used in the flat barbell bench press. Visualize a bar passing through both dumbbell handles: The lowest position of the dumbbells is where the imaginary bar would touch the chest at nipple level. Lifters performing this exercise with the dumbbells in a neutral position can lower them farther, if desired, because the torso does not obstruct the path of the dumbbells.

☐ Do not arch the low back to raise the chest.

☐ Keep the head, torso, hips, and feet in a five-point body-contact position.

Downward Movement: Spotter

☐ Keep the hands near—but not touching—the lifter's forearms as the dumbbells descend.

☐ Slightly flex the torso (but keep the back flat) when following the dumbbells.

Upward Movement: Lifter

☐ Press the dumbbells upward at the same rate and very slightly toward each other to keep them under control.

☐ Maintain the same stationary five-point body-contact position; do not arch the low back or lift the buttocks or feet.

☐ Keep the wrists stiff, the forearms perpendicular to the floor, and the dumbbell handles in line with each other; do not allow the dumbbells to sway as they are raised.

☐ Continue pressing the dumbbells up until the elbows are fully extended. Keep the forearms nearly parallel to each other; the dumbbells can move toward each other over the chest, but do not clang them together.

☐ At the completion of the set, first slowly lower the dumbbells to the chest (armpit) area and then, one at a time, return the dumbbells to the floor in a controlled manner.

Upward Movement: Spotter

☐ Keep the hands near—but not touching—the lifter's forearms as the dumbbells ascend.

☐ Slightly extend the torso (but keep the back flat) when following the dumbbells.

Incline Dumbbell Bench Press

Starting Position: Lifter

☐ Before picking up the dumbbells, check the seat of the incline bench. If it is adjustable, move the seat to allow for the following conditions:

- The thighs are approximately parallel to the floor (with the feet flat).
- The body is low enough so that the head is at the top of the bench.
- The dumbbells will not hit the uprights of the racks (if they are present) during the exercise.

☐ Grasp two equal-weight dumbbells with a closed grip. Position the outside surface of the little-finger half of the dumbbells against the front of the thighs (the dumbbell handles will be parallel to each other).

☐ Sit on the seat of an incline bench with the dumbbells resting on the thighs.

☐ Lean back to place the head at the top of the bench. As the inclined position is achieved, first move the dumbbells to the chest (armpit) area and then signal the spotter for assistance to move them to an extended-elbow position above the neck and face with the forearms parallel to each other.

☐ Reposition the head, shoulders, buttocks, and feet to achieve a five-point body-contact position:

1. Head is placed firmly against the bench.
2. Shoulders and upper back are placed firmly and evenly against the bench.
3. Buttocks are placed evenly on the seat.
4. Right foot is flat on the floor.
5. Left foot is flat on the floor.

☐ The most common dumbbell position is with the dumbbell handles in line with each other with the palms facing out. Another option is to hold the dumbbells in a neutral position (i.e., parallel to each other with the palms facing each other).

☐ All repetitions begin from this extended-elbow position with the dumbbells supported over the neck and face.

Starting Position: Spotter

☐ Stand erect behind the head of the bench.

☐ Place the feet shoulder-width apart with the knees slightly flexed.

☐ Grasp the lifter's wrists.

☐ At the lifter's signal, assist with moving the dumbbells to a position over the lifter's neck and face.

☐ Release the lifter's wrists smoothly.

Downward Movement: Lifter

☐ Begin the exercise by lowering the dumbbells slowly and under control toward the chest. To maintain a stable body position on the bench, lower the dumbbells at the same rate.

☐ Keep the wrists stiff, the forearms perpendicular to the floor, and the dumbbell handles in line with each other. Minimize all forward-to-backward and side-to-side movement.

☐ Guide the dumbbells down and slightly out to the lateral side of the chest, near the armpits and in line with the upper one-third area of the chest (between the clavicles and the nipples).

☐ Usually, the lowest position of the dumbbells is a depth similar to that used in the incline barbell bench press. Visualize a bar passing through both dumbbell handles: The lowest position of the dumbbells is where the imaginary bar would touch the upper one-third area of the chest. Lifters performing this exercise with the dumbbells in a neutral position can lower them farther, if desired, because the torso does not obstruct the path of the dumbbells.

☐ Do not arch the low back to raise the chest.

☐ Keep the head, torso, hips, and feet in a five-point body-contact position.

Incline Dumbbell Bench Press

Starting positions   **Downward and upward movements**

Downward Movement: Spotter

☐ Keep the hands near—but not touching—the lifter's forearms as the dumbbells descend.

☐ Slightly flex the knees, hips, and torso and keep the back flat when following the dumbbells.

Upward Movement: Lifter

☐ Press the dumbbells upward at the same rate and very slightly backward. To keep them from falling forward (because of the angled torso position), press the dumbbells up over the shoulders (initially) and face (eventually) instead of out and away from the chest.

☐ Do not arch the low back, raise the hips, or push up with the legs (by trying to stand up); the body and feet should not move from their initial positions.

☐ Keep the wrists stiff, the forearms perpendicular to the floor, and the dumbbell handles in line with each other; do not allow the dumbbells to sway as they are raised.

☐ Continue pressing the dumbbells up until the elbows are fully extended. Keep the forearms nearly parallel to each other; the dumbbells can move toward each other over the chest, but do not clang them together.

☐ At the completion of the set, first slowly lower the dumbbells to the chest (armpit) area and then to the thighs; then, one at a time, return the dumbbells to the floor in a controlled manner.

Upward Movement: Spotter

☐ Keep the hands near—but not touching—the lifter's forearms as the dumbbells ascend.

☐ Slightly extend the knees, hips, and torso and keep the back flat when following the dumbbells.

Flat Bench Press (Smith Machine)

Before loading the bar, lie down on the bench to check the height of the bar in relation to the body. When lying in a five-point body-contact position and holding on to the bar (see the following description for proper technique), the elbows should be slightly to moderately flexed so the bar can be lifted out of the racked position by simultaneously extending the elbows and rotating the bar.

Starting Position

☐ Lie supine on a flat bench and position the body to achieve a five-point body-contact position:

    1. Head is placed firmly on the bench.

    2. Shoulders and upper back are placed firmly and evenly on the bench.

    3. Buttocks are placed evenly on the bench.

    4. Right foot is flat on the floor.

    5. Left foot is flat on the floor.

☐ Adjust the body on the bench to position the *chest* directly below the racked bar.

☐ Grasp the bar evenly with a closed and pronated grip, slightly wider than shoulder-width apart.

☐ Slightly (or moderately, depending on the machine) rotate the bar from the racked position to unhook the bar from the supporting pins. Move the bar to a position over the chest with the elbows fully extended. All repetitions begin from this position.

Starting position

Downward and upward movements

Downward Movement

- ☐ Begin the exercise by lowering the bar slowly and under control toward the chest.
- ☐ The elbows move down past the torso and slightly away from the body.
- ☐ Keep the wrists stiff and the forearms perpendicular to the floor and parallel to each other. The width of the grip will determine how parallel the forearms are to each other.
- ☐ Lower the bar to lightly touch the chest at approximately nipple level; do not bounce the bar on the chest or arch the low back to raise the chest to meet the bar.
- ☐ Keep the head, torso, hips, and feet in a five-point body-contact position.

Upward Movement

- ☐ Press the bar upward.
- ☐ Maintain the same stationary five-point body-contact position; do not arch the low back or lift the buttocks or feet.
- ☐ Keep the wrists stiff and the forearms perpendicular to the floor and parallel to each other.
- ☐ Continue pressing the bar up until the elbows are fully extended but not forcefully locked.
- ☐ At the completion of the set, slightly (or moderately, depending on the machine) flex the elbows to align the hooks of the bar with the supporting pins. Keep a grip on the bar until the hooks on both ends are fully caught on the supporting pins.

Vertical Chest Press (Machine)

Starting Position

☐ Before performing this exercise, check the height of the seat and adjust it to allow for the following conditions:

▪ The thighs are approximately parallel to the floor (with the feet flat).

▪ The body is in line with the handgrips (an imaginary line connecting both handgrips should cross the front of the chest at nipple height).

▪ The arms are positioned approximately parallel to the floor when the elbows are extended and holding on to the handgrips. (Take the pin out of the weight stack, sit in the machine, and push the handles forward to check the arm position at a certain seat height.)

☐ Sit on the seat and lean back to place the body in a five-point body-contact position:

1. Head is placed firmly against the vertical back pad.
2. Shoulders and upper back are placed firmly and evenly against the vertical back pad.
3. Buttocks are placed evenly on the seat.
4. Right foot is flat on the floor.
5. Left foot is flat on the floor.

Starting position

Backward and forward movements

□ Grasp the handles with a closed, pronated (or neutral, if desired) grip.

□ If the machine has a foot pedal, do the following:

    1. Use one foot to depress the pedal to move the handles forward.

    2. Grasp the handles and push them forward to full elbow extension.

    3. Slowly release the foot pedal and place the foot on the floor.

□ If there is no foot pedal, grasp the handles one at a time and push them forward to full elbow extension.

□ All repetitions begin from this position.

Backward Movement

□ Begin the exercise by allowing the handles to move toward the body slowly and under control.

□ Keep the wrists stiff; the arms will be approximately parallel to the floor if the seat was adjusted properly before beginning the exercise.

□ Guide the handles back to the chest; do not allow the handles to rapidly move backward to add a bounce to help with the next repetition.

□ Keep the head, torso, hips, and feet in a five-point body-contact position.

Forward Movement

□ Push the handles forward.

□ Maintain the same stationary five-point body-contact position; do not arch the low back, lift the buttocks, or contract the abdominals (to flex the torso forward).

□ Keep the wrists stiff and continue pushing the handles until the elbows are fully extended but not forcefully locked.

□ At the completion of the set, reverse the foot pedal procedure or guide the handles backward to their resting position by releasing the grip on one handle at a time.

UPPER BODY

Assisted Dip (Machine)

Starting Position

☐ Step up and place the feet on the foot supports of the machine and stand erect.

☐ Grasp the handles with a closed, neutral grip and extend the elbows to raise the body and place the knees on the knee pad with the legs next to each other.

☐ Support the body weight with the elbows fully extended but not forcefully locked and the torso hanging from the shoulders. The knees should remain on the knee pad.

☐ Slightly lean the torso forward, keeping the back flat. Increasing the forward lean will increase the stress on the pectoralis major and anterior deltoid muscles. Straightening the torso to a more vertical position will increase the stress on the triceps brachii muscle.

☐ All repetitions begin from this position.

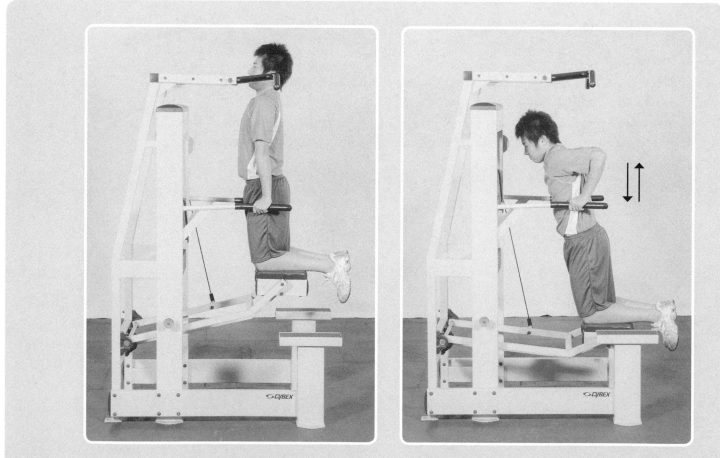

Starting position   **Downward and upward movements**

Downward Movement

☐ Begin the exercise by lowering the body slowly and under control by allowing the elbows to flex and the shoulders to extend.

☐ Maintain a slight forward lean of the torso, keeping the back flat.

☐ Continue to lower the body until the upper arms are parallel to the floor. Lowering the body past this point may cause injury to the shoulder joint.

Upward Movement

☐ Press the body up by extending the elbows and flexing the shoulders to return to the starting position.

☐ Maintain a slight forward lean of the torso, keeping the back flat.

☐ Continue to press the body up until the elbows are fully extended but not forcefully locked.

☐ At the completion of the set, remove the knees from the knee pad and step down to place the feet on the foot supports of the machine and then on the floor.

Chest (Single-Joint) Exercises

DVD 2

Name	Description of the concentric action	PREDOMINANT MUSCLES INVOLVED	
		Muscle group or body area	Muscles
Pec deck (machine)	Shoulder transverse (horizontal) adduction	Chest	Pectoralis major
		Shoulders	Anterior deltoid
	Scapular protraction (abduction)	Scapulae	Serratus anterior
		Chest	Pectoralis minor
✋ Flat dumbbell fly	Same as pec deck (machine)		
✋ Incline dumbbell fly	Same as pec deck (machine)		

✋ Denotes an exercise that requires a spotter.

Pec Deck (Machine)

Starting Position

☐ Before performing this exercise, check the height of the seat and adjust it to allow for the following conditions:

- The thighs are approximately parallel to the floor (with the feet flat).
- The shoulders are slightly above the bottom of the forearm pads (or in line with the elbow pads, depending on the type of machine).
- The upper arms are parallel to the floor (or slightly above) when the elbows are flexed to 90 degrees with the hands holding on to the handles. (Take the pin out of the weight stack, sit in the machine, and squeeze the handles together to check the arm position at a certain seat height.) In some machines, the back pad may be angled backward slightly or moderately.

☐ Sit on the seat and lean back to place the body in a five-point body-contact position:

1. Head is placed firmly against the vertical back pad.
2. Shoulders and upper back are placed firmly and evenly against the vertical back pad.
3. Buttocks are placed evenly on the seat.
4. Right foot is flat on the floor.
5. Left foot is flat on the floor.

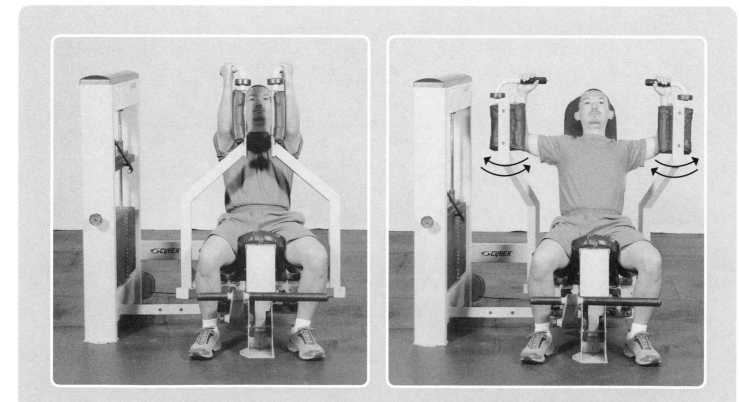

Starting position   **Backward and forward movements**

☐ Grasp the handles with

- a closed, pronated grip;
- the elbows flexed to 90 degrees; and
- the forearms pressed against the small vertical pads near the handgrips. (If the machine has elbow pads, press the inside of the elbows against them.)

☐ If the machine has a foot pedal, do the following:

1. Use one foot to depress the pedal to move the handles forward.
2. Grasp the handles and squeeze them together in front of the face.
3. Slowly release the foot pedal and place the foot on the floor.

☐ If there is no foot pedal, grasp the handles one at a time and bring them together in front of the face.

☐ All repetitions begin from this position.

Backward Movement

☐ Begin the exercise by allowing both handles to swing out and back slowly and under control.

☐ Keep the wrists stiff, the forearms and elbows pressed against the arm pads, and the upper arms parallel to the floor (or slightly above).

☐ Guide the handles back to be in line with the chest and each other; do not rapidly swing the handles back to add momentum to help with the next repetition.

☐ Keep the head, torso, hips, and feet in a five-point body-contact position.

Forward Movement

☐ Move the handles out and then toward each other by squeezing the forearms and elbows together. Do not simply pull with the hands; use the entire arm to exert pressure against the pads to squeeze the handles together.

☐ Maintain the same stationary five-point body-contact position; do not arch the low back, lift the buttocks, flex the torso forward, or jerk the torso or head forward.

☐ Keep the wrists stiff, the forearms and elbows pressed against the arm pads, and the upper arms parallel to the floor.

☐ Continue squeezing the handles together until they meet in front of the face (or as far as they will move forward).

☐ At the completion of the set, reverse the foot pedal procedure or guide the handles backward by slightly twisting the body to each side to return each handle (one at a time) to its resting position.

Flat Dumbbell Fly

Starting Position: Lifter

☐ Grasp two equal-weight dumbbells with a closed grip. Position the outside surface of the little-finger half of the dumbbells against the front of the thighs (the dumbbell handles will be parallel to each other).

☐ Sit on one end of a flat bench with the dumbbells resting on the thighs.

☐ Lie back so the head rests on the other end of the bench. As the supine position is achieved, first move the dumbbells to the chest (armpit) area and then signal the spotter for assistance to move them to an extended-elbow position above the chest with the forearms parallel to each other.

☐ Reposition the head, shoulders, buttocks, and feet to achieve a five-point body-contact position:

    1. Head is placed firmly on the bench.

    2. Shoulders and upper back are placed firmly and evenly on the bench.

    3. Buttocks are placed evenly on the bench.

    4. Right foot is flat on the floor.

    5. Left foot is flat on the floor.

Starting positions

Downward and upward movements

☐ Rotate the dumbbells to place them in a neutral hand position with the handles parallel to each other with the elbows pointing out to the sides.

☐ Slightly flex the elbows and hold this flexed position throughout the exercise.

☐ All repetitions begin with the arms in this position with the dumbbells supported over the chest.

Starting Position: Spotter

☐ Get into a low (but still erect) body position very close to the head of the bench.

☐ To create a stable spotting position, get into a fully lunged position with one knee on the floor and the foot of the other leg ahead of the rear knee and flat on the floor.

☐ Grasp the lifter's wrists.

☐ At the lifter's signal, assist with moving the dumbbells to a position over the lifter's chest.

☐ Release the lifter's wrists smoothly.

Starting position
(without spotter shown)

Downward and upward movements
(without spotter shown)

Downward Movement: Lifter

☐ Begin the exercise by lowering the dumbbells slowly in wide arcs under control. No movement should occur at the elbow joints; movement should occur only at the shoulders. To maintain a stable body position on the bench, lower the dumbbells at the same rate.

☐ Keep the wrists stiff and the elbows locked in a slightly flexed position with the dumbbell handles parallel to each other throughout the movement.

☐ The hands, wrists, forearms, elbows, upper arms, and shoulders should stay nearly in the same vertical plane, perpendicular to the floor.

☐ The elbows should move from pointing *out to the sides* to pointing *toward the floor* during the downward movement phase.

☐ Continue to lower the dumbbells in wide arcs until they are level with the top of the chest.

☐ Keep the head, torso, hips, and feet in a five-point body-contact position.

Downward Movement: Spotter

☐ Keep the hands near—but not touching—the lifter's forearms as the dumbbells descend.

☐ Slightly flex the torso (but keep the back flat) when following the dumbbells.

Upward Movement: Lifter

☐ Raise the dumbbells upward in wide arcs under control; imagine hugging a very large tree trunk with the arms.

☐ Keep the wrists stiff and the elbows locked in a slightly flexed position.

☐ Maintain the same stationary five-point body-contact position; do not arch the low back, lift the buttocks or feet, or shrug the shoulders to help raise the dumbbells.

☐ The hands, wrists, forearms, elbows, upper arms, and shoulders should stay in nearly the same vertical plane during the upward movement phase.

☐ Continue raising the dumbbells until they are positioned over the chest in the starting position.

☐ At the completion of the set, first slowly lower the dumbbells to the chest (armpit) area and then, one at a time, return the dumbbells to the floor in a controlled manner.

Upward Movement: Spotter

☐ Keep the hands near—but not touching—the lifter's forearms as the dumbbells ascend.

☐ Slightly extend the torso (but keep the back flat) when following the dumbbells.

Incline Dumbbell Fly

Starting Position: Lifter

☐ Before picking up the dumbbells, check the seat of the incline bench. If it is adjustable, move the seat to allow for the following conditions:

- The thighs are approximately parallel to the floor (with the feet flat).
- The body is low enough so that the head is at the top of the bench.
- The dumbbells will not hit the uprights of the racks (if they are present) during the exercise.

☐ Grasp two equal-weight dumbbells with a closed grip. Position the outside surface of the little-finger half of the dumbbells against the front of the thighs (the dumbbell handles will be parallel to each other).

☐ Sit on the seat of an incline bench with the dumbbells resting on the thighs.

☐ Lean back to place the head at the top of the bench. As the inclined position is achieved, first move the dumbbells to the chest (armpit) area and then signal the spotter for assistance to move them to an extended-elbow position above the neck and face with the forearms parallel to each other.

☐ Reposition the head, shoulders, buttocks, and feet to achieve a five-point body-contact position:

1. Head is placed firmly against the bench.
2. Shoulders and upper back are placed firmly and evenly against the bench.
3. Buttocks are placed evenly on the seat.
4. Right foot is flat on the floor.
5. Left foot is flat on the floor.

☐ Rotate the dumbbells to place them in a neutral hand position with the handles parallel to each other with the elbows pointing out to the sides.

☐ Slightly flex the elbows and hold this flexed position throughout the exercise.

☐ All repetitions begin with the arms in this position and with the dumbbells supported over the neck and face.

Starting Position: Spotter

☐ Stand erect behind the head of the bench.

☐ Place the feet shoulder-width apart with the knees slightly flexed.

☐ Grasp the lifter's wrists.

☐ At the lifter's signal, assist with moving the dumbbells to a position over the lifter's neck and face.

☐ Release the lifter's wrists smoothly.

Downward Movement: Lifter

☐ Begin the exercise by lowering the dumbbells slowly in wide arcs under control. No movement should occur at the elbow joints; movement should occur only at the shoulders. To maintain a stable body position on the bench, lower the dumbbells at the same rate.

☐ Keep the wrists stiff and the elbows locked in a slightly flexed position with the dumbbell handles parallel to each other throughout the movement.

☐ The hands, wrists, forearms, elbows, upper arms, and shoulders should stay nearly in the same vertical plane, perpendicular to the floor (despite the inclined body position).

☐ The elbows should move from pointing *out to the sides* to pointing *toward the floor* during the downward movement phase.

☐ Continue to lower the dumbbells in wide arcs until they are level with the shoulders, not the chest. If the dumbbells' path is too low (i.e., toward the feet and away from the neck and face), they will be much more difficult to control.

☐ Keep the head, torso, hips, and feet in a five-point body-contact position.

Downward Movement: Spotter

☐ Keep the hands near—but not touching—the lifter's forearms as the dumbbells descend.

☐ Slightly flex the knees, hips, and torso and keep the back flat when following the dumbbells.

Incline Dumbbell Fly

Starting positions

Downward and upward movements

Upward Movement: Lifter

☐ Raise the dumbbells upward in wide arcs under control; imagine hugging a very large tree trunk with the arms.

☐ Keep the wrists stiff and the elbows locked in a slightly flexed position.

☐ Maintain the same stationary five-point body-contact position; do not arch the low back, lift the buttocks or feet, shrug the shoulders, or push up with the legs to help raise the dumbbells.

☐ The hands, wrists, forearms, elbows, upper arms, and shoulders should stay in nearly the same vertical plane during the upward movement phase.

☐ Continue raising the dumbbells until they are positioned over the neck and face in the starting position.

☐ At the completion of the set, first slowly lower the dumbbells to the chest (armpit) area and then to the thighs; then, one at a time, return the dumbbells to the floor in a controlled manner.

Upward Movement: Spotter

☐ Keep the hands near—but not touching—the lifter's forearms as the dumbbells ascend.

☐ Slightly extend the knees, hips, and torso and keep the back flat when following the dumbbells.

UPPER BODY

Back (Multijoint) Exercises

DVD 2

Name	Description of the concentric action	PREDOMINANT MUSCLES INVOLVED	
		Muscle group or body area	Muscles
Lat pulldown (machine)	Shoulder adduction	Upper back	Latissimus dorsi Teres major
	Scapular retraction (adduction)	Upper, middle back	Middle trapezius Rhomboids
	Shoulder extension	Back	Latissimus dorsi Teres major
		Shoulders	Posterior deltoid
	Elbow flexion	Upper arm (anterior)	Brachialis Biceps brachii Brachioradialis
Bent-over row	Same as lat pulldown (machine), but the concentric action does not include shoulder adduction		
One-arm dumbbell row	Same as lat pulldown (machine), but the concentric action does not include shoulder adduction		
Low-pulley seated row (machine)	Same as lat pulldown (machine), but the concentric action does not include shoulder adduction		
Seated row (machine)	Same as lat pulldown (machine), but the concentric action does not include shoulder adduction		

Lat Pulldown (Machine)

Starting Position

☐ Grasp the long bar with a closed, pronated grip. (Various bar attachments can be used for this exercise; most are 36 to 48 inches [91 to 122 cm] long with slightly angled ends.)

☐ A common grip width using the long bar involves placing the index finger on the outside bends of the bar. If the bar is entirely straight, then use a wider-than-shoulder-width grip spaced evenly on the bar.

☐ Pull the bar down and move into one of the following positions:

■ If a seat is attached to the machine, then sit down facing the weight stack with the legs under the thigh pads and the feet flat on the floor, if possible. (If the bench seat is adjustable, position the thighs approximately parallel to the floor with the feet flat on the floor.)

■ If there is not a seat attached to the machine, then kneel down on one knee, facing the machine, and under the top pulley. The foot of the other leg is placed ahead of the body, flat on the floor.

☐ The elbows should be fully extended with the selected load suspended above the remainder of the weight stack.

Starting position   **Downward and upward movements**

☐ Before beginning the exercise, slightly lean the torso backward and extend the neck to create a clear path for the bar to pass by the face as it is pulled down. This position will also reduce impingement stress on the shoulder joints. All repetitions begin from this position.

Downward Movement

☐ Begin the exercise by pulling down on the bar; the elbows should move down and back and the chest up and out as the bar is lowered.

☐ As the bar approaches the face, slightly extend the neck to place the head in line with the rest of the spinal column. This will prevent the bar from hitting the forehead, nose, or chin as it is lowered.

☐ Maintain the same stationary body position; do not jerk the torso or quickly lean back farther to help pull the bar down.

☐ Continue pulling the bar down and *toward the body* (not just down) until it lightly touches the clavicle and upper-chest area. The torso should still have a slight backward lean at the bottom bar position.

Upward Movement

☐ Guide the bar slowly and under control back up to the starting position; do not allow the bar to jerk the arms upward.

☐ Maintain the same backward torso lean and lower-body position.

☐ The elbows should be fully extended at the end of the upward movement phase.

☐ At the completion of the set, stand up slowly and guide the bar under control to its resting position.

Bent-Over Row

Starting Position

☐ Grasp the bar evenly with a closed and pronated grip, wider than shoulder-width apart.

☐ Follow the preparatory body position and lifting guidelines (see introduction) to lift the bar off the floor to a position at the front of the thighs. The body should be fully erect before moving into the flexed torso position of the bent-over row.

☐ Place the feet shoulder-width apart (or slightly wider) with the knees slightly flexed.

☐ Flex the torso forward to be slightly above parallel to the floor while maintaining the same flexed knee position.

☐ Pull the shoulders back, push the chest out, and extend the neck slightly to create a flat or slightly concave (not rounded) back position. Do not attempt to look up at the ceiling; just focus on the floor a short distance ahead of the feet.

☐ Allow the bar to hang at full elbow extension; adjust the amount of knee and torso flexion so the weight plates are not touching the floor. All repetitions begin from this position.

Starting position   **Upward and downward movements**

Upward Movement

☐ Begin the exercise by pulling the bar up toward the torso; the elbows should point away from the sides of the body with the wrists kept straight. Do not curl the bar upward.

☐ Maintain the same stationary body position; do not shrug the shoulders, swing the body (i.e., extend the spine), hyperextend the neck, extend the knees, or rise up on the toes to help raise the bar upward.

☐ Continue pulling the bar up until it touches the sternum or upper abdomen. At the highest bar position, the elbows will be higher than the torso (when seen from the side).

Downward Movement

☐ Lower the bar slowly and under control to the starting position; do not flex the torso forward, extend the knees, or allow the body's weight to shift toward the toes.

☐ Maintain the same stationary torso, flat back, and flexed knee positions with the feet flat on the floor.

☐ The elbows should be fully extended at the end of the downward movement phase.

☐ At the completion of the set, slowly flex the hips and knees at the same rate to squat down and return the bar to the floor in a controlled manner.

One-Arm Dumbbell Row

Starting Position

☐ Stand on the right side of a flat bench (with the body perpendicular, not parallel, to the length of the bench) with a dumbbell on the floor next to the right foot.

☐ Kneel on the bench with the left leg and lean forward to place the left hand on the bench in front of the left knee. Place the hand far enough ahead of the knee on the bench so that the left arm and left thigh are approximately parallel to each other.

☐ Move the right foot closer to the side of the bench with the toes pointing ahead. The inside of the right thigh or knee should be very close to the right side of the bench.

☐ Slightly flex the right knee and maintain this flexed position during the exercise.

☐ Reach down with the right hand and grasp the dumbbell with a closed, neutral grip.

☐ Reposition both hips, the right knee, and the left elbow to place the torso approximately parallel to the floor with the dumbbell hanging down at full elbow extension.

☐ Pull the shoulders back, push the chest out, and slightly extend the neck to create a flat back position. Do not attempt to look up at the ceiling; just focus on the floor a short distance ahead of the feet.

Starting position   **Upward and downward movements**

☐ Allow the dumbbell to hang at full elbow extension. All repetitions begin from this position.

Upward Movement

☐ Begin the exercise by pulling the dumbbell up toward the torso; the upper right arm and elbow should be kept near the side of the body with the wrist straight. Do not curl the dumbbell upward or inward.

☐ Maintain the same stationary body position; do not swing or jerk the upper body upward to help raise the dumbbell.

☐ Continue pulling the dumbbell up until it touches the right side of the outer chest or rib cage area. At the highest dumbbell position, the right elbow will be higher than the torso (when seen from the side).

Downward Movement

☐ Lower the dumbbell slowly and under control to the starting position; do not allow the dumbbell to jerk the arm down.

☐ Maintain the same stationary torso, flat back, and flexed right knee positions with the right foot flat on the floor.

☐ After completing a set with the right arm, set the dumbbell on the floor, stand on the left side of the bench, and repeat the procedure using the left arm.

Low-Pulley Seated Row (Machine)

Starting Position

☐ Sit on the floor (or on the long seat pad, if one is present) facing the machine.

☐ Place the feet on the machine frame or foot supports.

☐ Flex the knees and hips to reach forward and grasp the handles with a closed, neutral grip. (Various attachments can be used for this exercise; one of the most common is a triangular-shaped double handle that places the hands in a neutral grip.)

☐ Pull the handles back and sit in an erect seated position with the torso perpendicular to the floor, knees slightly flexed, and feet and legs parallel to each other.

☐ The elbows should be fully extended and the arms parallel to the floor (or slightly below) with the selected load suspended above the remainder of the weight stack. All repetitions begin from this position.

Backward Movement

☐ Begin the exercise by pulling the handles toward the abdomen. The elbows should stay relatively near or next to the sides of the torso, *not* pointing directly out to the sides.

☐ Maintain the same stationary body position; do not jerk the torso, extend the knees, or quickly lean back farther to help pull the handles.

☐ Continue pulling the handles until the forearms or wrists press against the torso or until the handles (or bar, depending on what attachment is used) touch the abdomen.

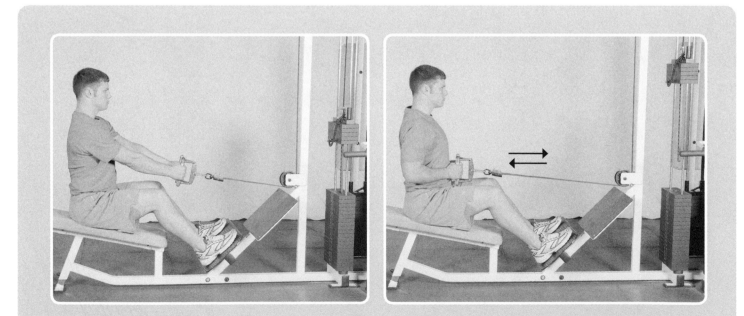

Starting position   **Backward and forward movements**

Forward Movement

☐ Guide the handles slowly and under control back to the starting position; do not allow the handles to jerk the arms forward.

☐ Maintain the same stationary torso and flexed knee position.

☐ The elbows should be fully extended at the end of the forward movement phase.

☐ At the completion of the set, slowly flex the knees and hips farther to move forward and return the handles to the resting position.

Seated Row (Machine)

Starting Position

☐ Before performing this exercise, check the height of the seat and position of the chest pad and adjust them to allow for the following conditions:
  - ■ The thighs are approximately parallel to the floor (with the feet flat or in the foot supports).
  - ■ The torso is perpendicular to the floor when sitting erect with the torso against the chest pad.
  - ■ The arms are approximately parallel to the floor when holding on to the handles.

☐ Sit erect with the feet flat on the floor or in the foot supports, and press the torso against the chest pad.

☐ Use one foot to depress the pedal to move the handles backward.

☐ Grasp the handles with a closed, pronated (or neutral, if desired) grip and then reposition the body to achieve the seated erect torso position.

☐ Slowly release the foot pedal and place the foot on the floor or in the foot support.

☐ The elbows should be fully extended and the arms approximately parallel to the floor with the selected load suspended above the remainder of the weight stack. All repetitions begin from this position.

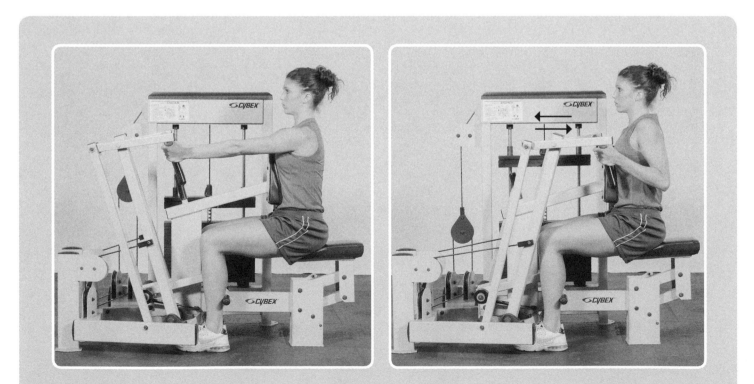

Starting position   **Backward and forward movements**

Backward Movement

☐ Begin the exercise by pulling the handles toward the torso, chest, upper abdomen, or lower abdomen, depending on the type of machine. The elbows should stay relatively near or next to the sides of the torso, *not* pointing directly out to the sides (but this depends on what handles are used).

☐ Maintain the same stationary body position; do not quickly lean back farther to help pull the handles.

☐ Continue pulling the handles until the forearms or wrists press against the torso or until the handles touch the torso.

Forward Movement

☐ Allow the handles to move slowly and under control to the starting position; do not allow the handles to jerk the arms forward.

☐ Maintain the same stationary torso position.

☐ The elbows should be fully extended at the end of the forward movement phase.

☐ At the completion of the set, reverse the foot pedal procedure to guide the handles back to the resting position.

Back (Single-Joint) Exercises

DVD 2

| | | PREDOMINANT MUSCLES INVOLVED | |
Name	Description of the concentric action	Muscle group or body area	Muscles
🖐 Barbell pullover	Shoulder extension	Back	Latissimus dorsi Teres major
	Scapular protraction (abduction)	Scapulae	Serratus anterior
		Chest	Pectoralis minor

🖐 Denotes an exercise that requires a spotter.

Barbell Pullover

Starting Position: Lifter

☐ Sit on one end of a flat bench and then lie back so the head rests on the other end of the bench.

☐ Position the head, shoulders, buttocks, and feet to achieve a five-point body-contact position:

1. Head is placed firmly on the bench.
2. Shoulders and upper back are placed firmly and evenly on the bench.
3. Buttocks are placed evenly on the bench.
4. Right foot is flat on the floor.
5. Left foot is flat on the floor.

☐ Signal the spotter to pick up the bar off the floor.

☐ Grasp the bar with a closed, pronated grip.

☐ Move the bar to an extended-elbow position above the chest with the forearms parallel to each other.

☐ Externally rotate the arms slightly so the elbows point away from the face (toward the knees) and moderately flex the elbows and hold this flexed position throughout the exercise. These two changes in the arm and elbow positions will result in the upper arms *not* being perpendicular to the floor; they will be moderately angled away from the face (toward the knees). All repetitions begin from this position.

Starting Position: Spotter

☐ Stand erect behind the head of the bench.

☐ Place the feet shoulder-width apart with the knees slightly flexed.

☐ Grasp the bar with a closed and alternated grip.

☐ Hand the bar to the lifter.

☐ Guide the bar to a position over the lifter's chest.

☐ Release the bar smoothly.

Downward Movement: Lifter

☐ Begin the exercise by lowering the bar in an arc over the face and then behind the head slowly and under control. A little movement can occur at the elbow joints; most of the movement should occur at the shoulders.

☐ Keep the wrists stiff and the arms parallel to each other.

☐ Continue to lower the bar behind the head until the shoulders are in a fully flexed position.

☐ Do not arch the low back as the bar is lowered.

☐ Keep the head, torso, hips, and feet in a five-point body-contact position.

Downward Movement: Spotter

☐ Keep the hands in the supinated grip position close to—but not touching—the bar as it descends.

☐ Slightly flex the knees, hips, and torso and keep the back flat when following the bar.

Upward Movement: Lifter

☐ Pull the bar upward in an arc by extending the shoulders, not the elbows (they should remain in the same moderately flexed position).

☐ Maintain the same stationary five-point body-contact position; do not lift the head.

☐ Keep the wrists stiff and the arms parallel to each other.

☐ Continue pulling the bar until it is positioned over the chest in the starting position.

☐ At the completion of the set, signal the spotter to take the bar, but keep a firm grip until the spotter gains full control of the bar.

Upward Movement: Spotter

☐ Keep the hands in the supinated grip position close to—but not touching—the bar as it ascends.

☐ Slightly extend the knees, hips, and torso and keep the back flat when following the bar.

☐ At the lifter's signal after the set is completed, stand up and grasp the bar with a closed and alternated grip, take it from the lifter, and set it on the floor.

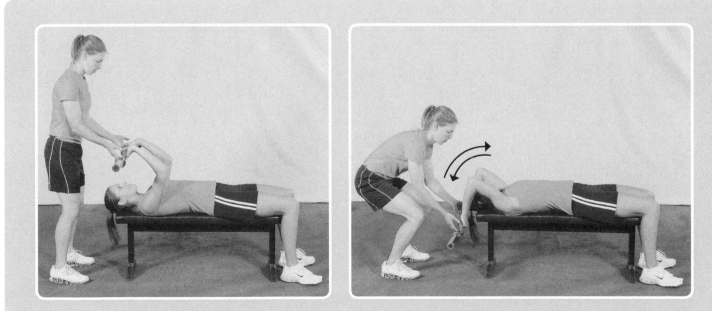

Starting positions   **Downward and upward movements**

Shoulder (Multijoint) Exercises

DVD 2

Name	Description of the concentric action	PREDOMINANT MUSCLES INVOLVED	
		Muscle group or body area	Muscles
Shoulder press (machine)	Shoulder abduction	Shoulders	Anterior and medial deltoids
	Scapular protraction (abduction)	Upper shoulders and upper back	Trapezius
		Scapulae	Serratus anterior
	Elbow extension	Upper arm (posterior)	Triceps brachii
✋ Seated barbell shoulder press	Same as shoulder press (machine)		
✋ Seated dumbbell shoulder press	Same as shoulder press (machine)		
Upright row	Shoulder abduction	Shoulders	Anterior, medial, and posterior deltoids
	Scapular protraction (abduction)	Upper shoulders and upper back	Trapezius
		Scapulae	Serratus anterior
	Elbow flexion	Upper arm (anterior)	Brachialis Biceps brachii Brachioradialis

✋ Denotes an exercise that requires a spotter.

Shoulder Press (Machine)

Starting Position

☐ Before performing this exercise, check the height of the seat and adjust it to allow for the following conditions:

■ The thighs are approximately parallel to the floor (with the feet flat).

■ The body is in line with the handgrips. (An imaginary line connecting both handgrips should cross *not lower than* the *top* of the shoulders or base of the neck.)

■ The body is low enough that the head is in contact with the pad at the top of the bench.

☐ Sit on the seat and lean back to place the body in a five-point body-contact position:

1. Head is placed firmly against the vertical back pad.
2. Shoulders and upper back are placed firmly and evenly against the vertical back pad.
3. Buttocks are placed evenly on the seat.
4. Right foot is flat on the floor.
5. Left foot is flat on the floor.

Starting position

Upward and downward movements

☐ Grasp the handles with a closed, pronated (or neutral, if desired) grip. All repetitions begin from this position.

Upward Movement

☐ Begin the exercise by pressing the handles upward.

☐ Maintain the same stationary five-point body-contact position; do not arch the low back, raise the hips, push upward with the legs (by trying to stand up), or tilt the head backward.

☐ Keep the wrists stiff and the forearms approximately parallel to each other and continue pressing the handles until the elbows are fully extended but not forcefully locked.

Downward Movement

☐ Allow the handles to move slowly and under control back to the starting position; do not flex the torso forward as the handles are lowered.

☐ Maintain the same stationary five-point body-contact position; do not allow the handles to rapidly move downward to add a bounce to help with the next repetition.

☐ At the completion of the set, return the handles to the resting position.

Seated Barbell Shoulder Press

Starting Position: Lifter

☐ Before performing this exercise, check the seat of the shoulder press bench. If it is adjustable, move the seat to allow for the following conditions:
- ■ The thighs are approximately parallel to the floor (with the feet flat). The head is lower than the racked bar and resting at the top of the bench (if the bench has a long vertical back pad; some benches have a back pad height of a standard chair instead).
- ■ The bar can be lifted off and returned to the supporting pins or ledge without hitting the top of the head (the seat is too high) or requiring the use of the legs to help reach the racks (the seat is too low).

☐ Sit on the seat in a five-point body-contact position:
1. Head is placed firmly against the vertical back pad (if the back pad is long enough).
2. Shoulders and upper back are placed firmly and evenly against the vertical back pad.
3. Buttocks are placed evenly on the seat.
4. Right foot is flat on the floor.
5. Left foot is flat on the floor.

☐ Grasp the bar evenly with a closed and pronated grip, slightly wider than shoulder-width apart.

☐ Signal the spotter for assistance to move the bar off the racks to a position over the head with the elbows fully extended. This is the liftoff. All repetitions begin from this position.

Starting Position: Spotter

☐ Stand erect behind the back of the bench.

☐ Place the feet shoulder-width apart with the knees slightly flexed.

☐ Grasp the bar with a closed and alternated grip inside the lifter's hands.

☐ At the lifter's signal, assist with moving the bar off the racks.

☐ Guide the bar to a position over the lifter's head.

☐ Release the bar smoothly.

Downward Movement: Lifter

☐ Begin the exercise by lowering the bar slowly and under control.

☐ Keep the wrists stiff and the forearms perpendicular to the floor and parallel to each other. The width of the grip will determine how parallel the forearms are to each other.

☐ Lower the bar directly in front of the face; do not let the bar hit the forehead or nose as it is lowered.

☐ Continue to lower the bar until it lightly touches the clavicles. Do not bounce the bar on the shoulders or arch the low back.

☐ Keep the head, torso, hips, and feet in a five-point body-contact position.

Downward Movement: Spotter

☐ Keep the hands in the alternated grip position close to—but not touching—the bar as it descends.

☐ Slightly flex the knees, hips, and torso and keep the back flat when following the bar.

Upward Movement: Lifter

☐ Press the bar straight upward until it passes by the forehead; at that time, press it up *and* very slightly backward to keep it under control.

☐ Do not arch the low back, raise the hips, or push up with the legs (by trying to stand up); the body and feet should not move from their initial positions.

☐ Keep the wrists stiff and the forearms perpendicular to the floor and parallel to each other.

☐ Continue pressing the bar up until the elbows are fully extended (but not forcefully locked) with the bar overhead.

☐ At the completion of the set, signal the spotter for assistance to rack the bar, but keep a grip on the bar until both ends are secure and motionless on the supporting pins or ledge.

Starting positions　　　　　**Downward and upward movements**

UPPER BODY

Upward Movement: Spotter

☐ Keep the hands in the alternated grip position close to—but not touching—the bar as it ascends.

☐ Slightly extend the knees, hips, and torso and keep the back flat when following the bar.

☐ At the lifter's signal after the set is completed, grasp the bar with an alternated grip inside the lifter's hands.

☐ Guide the bar back onto the rack.

☐ Keep a grip on the bar until it is secure and motionless on the supporting pins or ledge.

Seated Dumbbell Shoulder Press

Starting Position: Lifter

☐ Before picking up the dumbbells, check the seat of the bench. If it is adjustable, move the seat to allow for the following conditions:

- The thighs are approximately parallel to the floor (with the feet flat).
- The body is low enough so that the head is at the top of the bench (if the bench has a long vertical back pad; some benches have a back pad height of a standard chair instead).
- The dumbbells will not hit the uprights of the racks (if they are present) during the exercise.

☐ Grasp two equal-weight dumbbells with a closed grip. Position the outside surface of the little-finger half of the dumbbells against the front of the thighs (the dumbbell handles will be parallel to each other).

☐ Sit on the seat with the dumbbells resting on the thighs. Move the dumbbells to the outside of the shoulders so that the dumbbell handles are level with the top of the shoulders or the base of the neck.

☐ Reposition the head, shoulders, buttocks, and feet to achieve a five-point body-contact position:

1. Head is placed firmly against the vertical back pad (if the back pad is long enough; the photos show a short vertical back pad).
2. Shoulders and upper back are placed firmly and evenly against the vertical back pad.
3. Buttocks are placed evenly on the seat.
4. Right foot is flat on the floor.
5. Left foot is flat on the floor.

☐ The most common dumbbell position is with the dumbbell handles in line with each other with the palms facing out. Another option is to hold the dumbbells in a neutral position (i.e., parallel to each other with the palms facing each other).

☐ All repetitions begin from this position.

Starting Position: Spotter

☐ Stand erect behind the back of the bench.

☐ Place the feet shoulder-width apart with the knees slightly flexed.

☐ Grasp the lifter's wrists.

☐ At the lifter's signal, assist with moving the dumbbells to a position outside the shoulders.

☐ Release the lifter's wrists smoothly.

Upward Movement: Lifter

☐ Begin the exercise by pressing the dumbbells upward at the same rate and very slightly toward each other to keep them under control.

☐ Maintain the same stationary five-point body-contact position; do not arch the low back, raise the hips, push upward with the legs (by trying to stand up), or tilt the head backward.

☐ Keep the wrists stiff, the forearms perpendicular to the floor, and the dumbbell handles in line with each other; do not allow the dumbbells to sway as they are raised.

☐ The hands, elbows, and shoulders should be in the same vertical plane.

☐ Continue pressing the dumbbells up until the elbows are fully extended. Keep the forearms nearly parallel to each other; the dumbbells can move toward each other over the head, but do not clang them together.

Upward Movement: Spotter

☐ Keep the hands near—but not touching—the lifter's forearms as the dumbbells ascend.

☐ Slightly extend the knees, hips, and torso and keep the back flat when following the dumbbells.

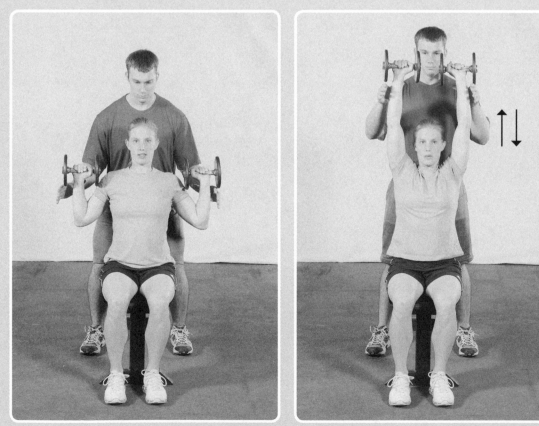

Seated Dumbbell Shoulder Press

Starting positions   **Upward and downward movements**

Downward Movement: Lifter

- ☐ Lower the dumbbells slowly and under control to the starting position. To maintain a stable body position on the bench, lower the dumbbells at the same rate.

- ☐ Keep the wrists stiff, the forearms perpendicular to the floor, and the dumbbell handles in line with each other.

- ☐ Continue to lower the dumbbells until they are level with the top of the shoulders or the base of the neck; do not bounce the dumbbells on the shoulders or shrug the shoulders to meet the dumbbells.

- ☐ Keep the head, torso, hips, and feet in a five-point body-contact position.

- ☐ At the completion of the set, slowly lower the dumbbells to the thighs; then, one at a time, return the dumbbells to the floor in a controlled manner.

Downward Movement: Spotter

- ☐ Keep the hands near—but not touching—the lifter's forearms as the dumbbells descend.

- ☐ Slightly flex the knees, hips, and torso and keep the back flat when following the dumbbells.

Upright Row

Starting Position

☐ Grasp the bar evenly with a closed and pronated grip, narrower than shoulder width but not closer than a position where the thumbs, when extended along the bar, could touch each other.

☐ Follow the preparatory body position and lifting guidelines (see introduction) to lift the bar off the floor to a position at the front of the thighs.

☐ Place the feet shoulder- or hip-width apart with the knees slightly flexed (slightly more than what appears in the photos), torso erect, shoulders held back, and eyes focused ahead.

☐ Allow the bar to hang at full elbow extension. All repetitions begin from this position.

Upward Movement

☐ Begin the exercise by pulling the bar up along the abdomen and chest by abducting the shoulders and flexing the elbows.

☐ Keep the elbows pointed out to the sides as the bar brushes against the body. Do not curl the bar upward.

Starting position　　　　　　　**Upward and downward movements**

☐ Maintain the same stationary body position; do not shrug the shoulders, swing the body (i.e., hyperextend the spine), hyperextend the neck, extend the knees, or rise up on the toes to help raise the bar upward.

☐ Continue pulling the bar up until it reaches the area between the bottom of the sternum and the chin (depending on arm length and shoulder flexibility). At the highest bar position, the elbows should be level with or slightly higher than the shoulders and wrists.

Downward Movement

☐ Lower the bar slowly and under control to the starting position; do not flex the torso forward, bounce the bar on the thighs at the bottom position, or allow the body's weight to shift toward the toes.

☐ Maintain the same stationary body position with the feet flat on the floor.

☐ The elbows should be fully extended at the end of the downward movement phase.

☐ At the completion of the set, slowly flex the hips and knees at the same rate (to keep an erect torso position) to squat down and return the bar to the floor in a controlled manner.

Shoulder (Single-Joint) Exercises

DVD 2

Name	Description of the concentric action	PREDOMINANT MUSCLES INVOLVED	
		Muscle group or body area	Muscles
Front shoulder raise	Shoulder flexion	Shoulders	*Anterior deltoid*
Lateral shoulder raise	Shoulder abduction	Shoulders	*Medial deltoid*
Lateral shoulder raise (machine)	Same as lateral shoulder raise		
Bent-over shoulder raise	Shoulder transverse (horizontal) abduction	Shoulders	*Posterior deltoid*
Barbell shoulder shrug	Shoulder girdle elevation	Shoulder girdle	Upper trapezius

The portion of the deltoid muscle group most emphasized in these exercises is in *bolded italics*.

Front Shoulder Raise

Starting Position

☐ Grasp two equal-weight dumbbells with a closed grip.

☐ Follow the preparatory body position and lifting guidelines (see introduction) to lift the dumbbells off the floor to a position next to the thighs.

☐ Place the feet shoulder- or hip-width apart with the knees slightly flexed, torso erect, shoulders held back, and eyes focused ahead.

☐ Move the dumbbells to the front of the thighs and position them with the palms facing the thighs (this creates a pronated grip position).

☐ Slightly flex the elbows and hold this flexed position throughout the exercise. All repetitions begin from this position.

Upward Movement

☐ Begin the exercise by raising one dumbbell up directly in front of the body. No movement should occur at the elbow joint; movement should occur only at the shoulder. Also, the nonexercising arm should be kept stationary at the front of the thigh (only one arm is involved at a time).

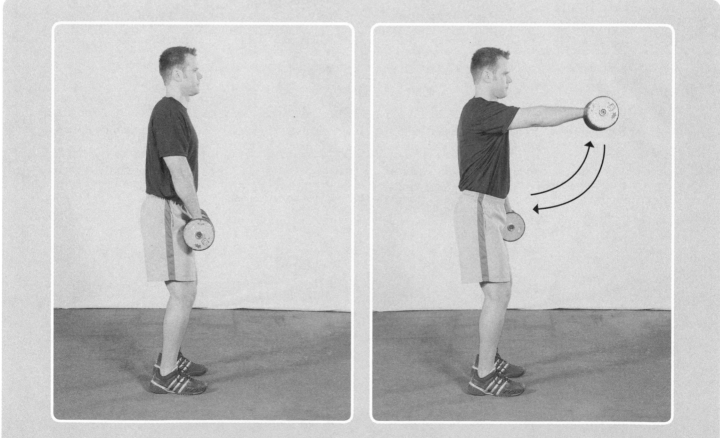

Starting position   **Upward and downward movements**

☐ Keep the wrist stiff and the elbow locked in a slightly flexed position; maintain a pronated grip on the dumbbell.

☐ The upper arm, elbow, forearm, and dumbbell should stay in nearly the same vertical plane during the upward movement phase. Neither the hand (dumbbell) nor the upper arm (elbow) should rise up ahead of or higher than the other.

☐ Maintain the same stationary body position; do not shrug the shoulders, swing the body (i.e., hyperextend the spine), extend the knees, or rise up on the toes to help raise the dumbbell.

☐ Continue raising the dumbbell until the arm is parallel to the floor or approximately level with the shoulder.

Downward Movement

☐ Lower the dumbbell slowly and under control to the starting position; do not flex the torso forward, extend the knees, or allow the body's weight to shift toward the toes.

☐ Keep the wrist stiff and the elbow locked in a slightly flexed position.

☐ Maintain the same stationary body position; do not allow the dumbbell to jerk the arm down.

☐ Continue to lower the dumbbell until it returns to the front of the thigh; do not bounce the dumbbell on the thigh to help with the next repetition.

☐ The nonexercising arm should be kept stationary at the front of the thigh.

☐ Repeat the upward and downward movement phases with the other arm; the arm just used should remain stationary until the dumbbell in the other hand returns back to the starting position. Continue to alternate the arms to complete the set.

☐ At the completion of the set, slowly flex the hips and knees at the same rate (to keep an erect torso position) to squat down and return the dumbbells to the floor in a controlled manner.

Lateral Shoulder Raise

Starting Position

☐ Grasp two equal-weight dumbbells with a closed grip.

☐ Follow the preparatory body position and lifting guidelines (see introduction) to lift the dumbbells off the floor to a position next to the thighs.

☐ Place the feet shoulder- or hip-width apart with the knees slightly flexed, torso erect, shoulders held back, and eyes focused ahead.

☐ Move the dumbbells to the front of the thighs and position them with the palms facing each other (this creates a neutral grip position).

☐ Slightly flex the elbows and hold this flexed position throughout the exercise. All repetitions begin from this position.

Upward Movement

☐ Begin the exercise by raising the dumbbells up and out to the sides. No movement should occur at the elbow joints; movement should occur only at the shoulders.

☐ Keep the wrists stiff and the elbows locked in a slightly flexed position; maintain a neutral grip on the dumbbells.

☐ The upper arms, elbows, forearms, and dumbbells should stay nearly in the same vertical plane and rise together.

Starting position   **Upward and downward movements**

☐ Maintain the same stationary body position; do not shrug the shoulders, swing the body (i.e., hyperextend the spine), extend the knees, or rise up on the toes to help raise the dumbbells.

☐ Continue raising the dumbbells until the arms are parallel to the floor or approximately level with the shoulders.

Downward Movement

☐ Lower the dumbbells slowly and under control to the starting position; do not flex the torso forward, extend the knees, or allow the body's weight to shift toward the toes.

☐ Keep the wrists stiff and the elbows locked in a slightly flexed position.

☐ Maintain the same stationary body position; do not allow the dumbbells to jerk the arms down.

☐ Continue to lower the dumbbells until they return to the front of the thighs; do not bounce the dumbbells on the thighs to help with the next repetition.

☐ At the completion of the set, slowly flex the hips and knees at the same rate (to keep an erect torso position) to squat down and return the dumbbells to the floor in a controlled manner.

Lateral Shoulder Raise (Machine)

Starting Position

☐ Before performing this exercise, check the height of the seat and adjust it to allow for the following conditions:

- The thighs are approximately parallel to the floor (with the feet flat).
- The shoulders are in line with the axis (or axes) of rotation of the machine.
- The body is low enough that the head is in contact with the pad at the top of the bench (if the bench has a long vertical back pad; some benches have a back pad height of a standard chair instead).

☐ Sit on the seat and place the body in a five-point body-contact position:

1. Head is placed firmly against the vertical back pad (if the back pad is long enough; the photos show a short vertical back pad).
2. Shoulders and upper back are placed firmly and evenly against the vertical back pad.
3. Buttocks are placed evenly on the seat.
4. Right foot is flat on the floor.
5. Left foot is flat on the floor.

Starting position   **Upward and downward movements**

☐ Flex the elbows to 90 degrees and place them at the sides or slightly in front of the body with the forearms pressed against the forearm pads.

☐ If handles are present, grasp them with a closed grip. All repetitions begin from this position.

Upward Movement

☐ Begin the exercise by raising the elbows and forearm pads up and out to the sides. No movement should occur at the elbow joints; movement should occur only at the shoulders.

☐ Keep the wrists stiff and the elbows locked at a 90-degree flexed position.

☐ The upper arms, elbows, and forearms should rise together.

☐ Maintain the same stationary five-point body-contact position; do not shrug the shoulders, arch the low back, raise the hips, push upward with the legs (by trying to stand up), or tilt the head backward.

☐ Continue raising the elbows and forearm pads until the upper arms are parallel to the floor or approximately level with the shoulders.

Downward Movement

☐ Allow the elbows and forearm pads to move slowly and under control back to the starting position; do not flex the torso forward as the handles are lowered.

☐ Keep the wrists stiff and the elbows locked at a 90-degree flexed position.

☐ Maintain the same stationary five-point body-contact position; do not allow the forearm pads to move down rapidly to add a bounce to help with the next repetition.

☐ At the completion of the set, return the forearm pads to the resting position.

Bent-Over Shoulder Raise

Starting Position

☐ Grasp two equal-weight dumbbells with a closed grip.

☐ Follow the preparatory body position and lifting guidelines (see introduction) to lift the dumbbells off the floor to a position next to the thighs. The body should be fully erect before moving into the flexed torso position of the bent-over shoulder raise.

☐ Place the feet shoulder- or hip-width apart with the knees slightly flexed.

☐ Flex the torso forward to slightly above parallel to the floor while maintaining the same flexed knee position.

☐ Pull the shoulders back, push the chest out, and extend the neck slightly to create a flat or slightly concave (not rounded) back position. Do not attempt to look up at the ceiling; just focus on the floor a short distance ahead of the feet.

☐ Allow the dumbbells to hang at full elbow extension; adjust the amount of knee and torso flexion so the dumbbells are not touching the floor.

☐ Reposition the dumbbells in a neutral hand position with the handles parallel to each other and the elbows pointing out to the sides.

☐ Slightly flex the elbows and hold the flexed position throughout the exercise. All repetitions begin from this position.

Starting position

Upward and downward movements

Upward Movement

☐ Begin the exercise by raising the dumbbells up and out to the sides. No movement should occur at the elbow joints; movement should occur only at the shoulders.

☐ Keep the wrists stiff and the elbows locked in a slightly flexed position; maintain a neutral grip on the dumbbells.

☐ The upper arms, elbows, forearms, and dumbbells should stay nearly in the same vertical plane (perpendicular to the body) during the upward movement phase. The elbows should rise together and ahead of and slightly higher than the dumbbells.

☐ Maintain the flat back, stationary torso, and flexed knee positions with the feet flat on the floor; do not swing the body (i.e., extend the spine), extend the knees, or rise up on the toes to help raise the dumbbells.

☐ Continue raising the dumbbells until the upper arms are approximately parallel to the floor or approximately level with the shoulders. At the highest position, the elbows will be slightly higher than the dumbbells.

Downward Movement

☐ Lower the dumbbells slowly and under control to the starting position; do not flex the torso forward, extend the knees, or allow the body's weight to shift toward the toes.

☐ Keep the wrists stiff and the elbows locked in a slightly flexed position.

☐ Maintain the flat back, stationary torso, and flexed knee positions with the feet flat on the floor.

☐ Continue to lower the dumbbells until they return to their hanging starting position; keep the dumbbell handles parallel to each other during the downward movement phase.

☐ At the completion of the set, slowly flex the hips and knees at the same rate to squat down and return the dumbbells to the floor in a controlled manner.

Barbell Shoulder Shrug

Starting Position

☐ Grasp the bar evenly with a closed and pronated (or alternated, if desired) grip, shoulder- or hip-width apart.

☐ Follow the preparatory body position and lifting guidelines (see introduction) to lift the bar off the floor to a position at the front of the thighs.

☐ Place the feet shoulder- or hip-width apart with the knees slightly flexed, torso erect, shoulders held back, and eyes focused ahead.

☐ Allow the bar to hang at full elbow extension. All repetitions begin from this position.

Upward Movement

☐ Begin the exercise by lifting the bar up along the thighs by elevating (shrugging) the shoulder girdle (shoulders).

☐ Keep the wrists stiff and the elbows fully extended.

☐ Maintain the same stationary body position; do not swing the body (i.e., hyperextend the spine), hyperextend the neck, extend the knees, or rise up on the toes to help raise the bar upward.

☐ Continue lifting the bar up until the shoulders are fully elevated.

Starting position

Upward and downward movements

Downward Movement

☐ Lower the bar slowly and under control to the starting position; do not flex the torso forward, bounce the bar on the thighs at the bottom position, flex the elbows, or allow the body's weight to shift toward the toes.

☐ Maintain the same stationary body position with the feet flat on the floor.

☐ At the completion of the set, slowly flex the hips and knees at the same rate (to keep an erect torso position) to squat down and return the bar to the floor in a controlled manner.

Biceps (Single-Joint) Exercises

DVD 2

Name	Description of the concentric action	PREDOMINANT MUSCLES INVOLVED	
		Muscle group or body area	Muscles
Barbell biceps curl	Elbow flexion	Upper arm (anterior)	Brachialis **_Biceps brachii_** Brachioradialis
Dumbbell biceps curl	Elbow flexion Forearm supination	Upper arm (anterior)	**_Brachialis_** **_Biceps brachii_** Brachioradialis
Hammer curl	Same as barbell biceps curl		**_Brachialis_** Biceps brachii Brachioradialis
Low-pulley biceps curl (machine)	Same as barbell biceps curl		Brachialis **_Biceps brachii_** Brachioradialis
Biceps curl (machine)	Same as barbell biceps curl		Brachialis **_Biceps brachii_** Brachioradialis

The elbow flexors emphasized in these exercises are in **_bolded italics_**.

Barbell Biceps Curl

This exercise commonly uses (but does not require) an EZ-bar, a short bar that is bent to create two distinct hand placements: an inside and an outside grip. Holding the bar to form an M with the bends allows the hands to grasp the bar evenly with a narrow, inside grip. Reversing the bar to create a W results in a wider, outside hand position. Either grip can be used. When performing this exercise with either an EZ-bar or a straight bar (shown in the photos), the upper arms must remain parallel.

Starting Position

☐ Grasp the bar evenly with a closed, supinated grip.

☐ Follow the preparatory body position and lifting guidelines (see introduction) to lift the bar off the floor to a position at the front of the thighs.

☐ A common grip width involves placing the hands on the bar so the arms touch the sides of the torso or hips and the little fingers are next to (and in contact with) the sides of the thighs.

☐ Place the feet shoulder- or hip-width apart with the knees slightly flexed, torso erect, shoulders held back, and eyes focused ahead.

☐ Allow the bar to hang at full elbow extension. All repetitions begin from this position.

Starting position

Upward and downward movements

Upward Movement

☐ Begin the exercise by raising the bar in an arc by flexing the arms at the elbows.

☐ Keep the wrists stiff and the upper arms stationary against the sides of the torso as the bar is raised; do not let them move forward or outward. No movement should occur at the shoulders; movement should occur only at the elbow joints.

☐ Maintain the same stationary body position; do not swing the body (i.e., hyperextend the spine), shrug the shoulders, hyperextend the neck, extend the knees, or rise up on the toes to help raise the bar upward.

☐ Continue flexing the elbows until the bar is near the anterior deltoids. If the elbows move forward at the highest bar position, then the elbows have flexed too far.

Downward Movement

☐ Lower the bar slowly and under control to the starting position by extending the elbows; do not bounce the bar on the thighs at the bottom position, flex the torso forward, extend the knees, or allow the body's weight to shift toward the toes.

☐ Keep the wrists stiff and the upper arms stationary against the sides of the torso.

☐ Maintain the same stationary body position with the feet flat on the floor.

☐ Continue to lower the bar until the elbows are fully extended but not forcefully locked.

☐ At the completion of the set, slowly flex the hips and knees at the same rate (to keep an erect torso position) to squat down and return the bar to the floor in a controlled manner.

Dumbbell Biceps Curl

Starting Position

☐ Grasp two equal-weight dumbbells with a closed, neutral grip.

☐ Follow the preparatory body position and lifting guidelines (see introduction) to lift the dumbbells off the floor to a position next to the thighs.

☐ A common arm position involves hanging the arms at the sides of the torso or hips with the palms facing the outer thighs.

☐ Place the feet shoulder- or hip-width apart with the knees slightly flexed, torso erect, shoulders held back, and eyes focused ahead.

☐ Allow the dumbbells to hang at full elbow extension. All repetitions begin from this position.

Upward Movement

☐ Begin the exercise by raising one dumbbell upward in an arc by flexing the arm at the elbow. The nonexercising arm should be kept stationary at the side of the thigh (only one arm is involved at a time).

☐ Keep the wrist stiff and the upper arm stationary against the side of the torso as the dumbbell is raised; do not let it move forward or outward. No movement should occur at the shoulder; movement should occur only at the elbow joint.

Starting position

Upward and downward movements

☐ Flex the elbow with a neutral hand position until the little-finger half of the dumbbell passes by the thigh and moves to the front of the body. When this occurs, begin to supinate the forearm and wrist by turning the hand outward.

☐ Maintain the same stationary body position; do not swing the body (i.e., hyperextend the spine), shrug the shoulders, hyperextend the neck, extend the knees, or rise up on the toes to help raise the dumbbell upward.

☐ Continue flexing the elbow and supinating the forearm and wrist until the dumbbell is near the anterior deltoid in a palms-up hand position. If the elbow moves forward at the highest dumbbell position, then the elbow has flexed too far.

Downward Movement

☐ Lower the dumbbell slowly and under control to the starting position by gradually pronating the forearm and wrist by turning the hand inward. Pronate sufficiently (and soon enough) to allow the dumbbell to pass to the outside of the thigh in a neutral position.

☐ Do not flex the torso forward, extend the knees, or allow the body's weight to shift toward the toes.

☐ Keep the wrist stiff and the upper arm stationary against the side of the torso.

☐ Maintain the same stationary body position with the feet flat on the floor.

☐ Continue to lower the dumbbell until the elbow is fully extended but not forcefully locked.

☐ The nonexercising arm should be kept stationary at the side of the thigh.

☐ Repeat the upward and downward movement phases with the other arm; the arm just used should remain stationary until the dumbbell in the other hand returns back to the starting position. Continue to alternate the arms to complete the set.

☐ At the completion of the set, slowly flex the hips and knees at the same rate (to keep an erect torso position) to squat down and return the dumbbells to the floor in a controlled manner.

Hammer Curl

Starting Position

☐ Grasp two equal-weight dumbbells with a closed, neutral grip.

☐ Follow the preparatory body position and lifting guidelines (see introduction) to lift the dumbbells off the floor to a position next to the thighs.

☐ A common arm position involves hanging the arms at the sides of the torso or hips with the palms facing the outer thighs.

☐ Place the feet shoulder- or hip-width apart with the knees slightly flexed, torso erect, shoulders held back, and eyes focused ahead.

☐ Allow the dumbbells to hang at full elbow extension. All repetitions begin from this position.

Upward Movement

☐ Begin the exercise by raising one dumbbell upward in an arc by flexing the arm at the elbow. The nonexercising arm should be kept stationary at the side of the thigh (only one arm is involved at a time).

☐ Keep the wrist stiff and the upper arm stationary against the side of the torso as the dumbbell is raised; do not let it move forward or outward. No movement should occur at the shoulder; movement should occur only at the elbow joint.

Starting position

Upward and downward movements

☐ The dumbbell remains in a neutral position as it is raised.

☐ Maintain the same stationary body position; do not swing the body (i.e., hyperextend the spine), shrug the shoulders, hyperextend the neck, extend the knees, or rise up on the toes to help raise the dumbbell upward.

☐ Continue flexing the elbow until the thumb half of the dumbbell is near the anterior deltoid in a neutral hand position. If the elbow moves forward at the highest dumbbell position, then the elbow has flexed too far.

Downward Movement

☐ Lower the dumbbell slowly and under control to the starting position with the handle in a neutral grip.

☐ Do not flex the torso forward, extend the knees, or allow the body's weight to shift toward the toes.

☐ Keep the wrist stiff and the upper arm stationary against the side of the torso.

☐ Maintain the same stationary body position with the feet flat on the floor.

☐ Continue to lower the dumbbell until the elbow is fully extended but not forcefully locked.

☐ The nonexercising arm should be kept stationary at the side of the thigh.

☐ Repeat the upward and downward movement phases with the other arm; the arm just used should remain stationary until the dumbbell in the other hand returns back to the starting position. Continue to alternate the arms to complete the set.

☐ At the completion of the set, slowly flex the hips and knees at the same rate (to keep an erect torso position) to squat down and return the dumbbells to the floor in a controlled manner.

Low-Pulley Biceps Curl (Machine)

Starting Position

☐ Stand approximately 18 inches (46 cm) away from and directly in front of a low-pulley station.

☐ Grasp the bar evenly with a closed, supinated grip.

☐ A common grip width involves placing the hands on the bar so the arms touch the sides of the torso or hips.

☐ Place the feet shoulder- or hip-width apart, with the knees slightly flexed, torso erect or leaning slightly backward, shoulders held back, and eyes focused ahead.

☐ Allow the bar to hang at full elbow extension. The hands and forearms will be slightly in front of the body because of the machine cable attachment. All repetitions begin from this position.

Upward Movement

☐ Begin the exercise by raising the bar in an arc by flexing the arms at the elbows.

Starting position   **Upward and downward movements**

☐ Keep the wrists stiff and the upper arms stationary against the sides of the torso as the bar is raised; do not let them move forward or outward. No movement should occur at the shoulders; movement should occur only at the elbow joints.

☐ Maintain the same stationary body position; do not swing the body (i.e., hyperextend the spine), shrug the shoulders, hyperextend the neck, extend the knees, or rise up on the toes to help raise the bar upward. The torso should be erect or leaning slightly backward to keep the body in a stable position throughout the exercise.

☐ Continue flexing the elbows until the bar is near the anterior deltoids. If the elbows move forward at the highest bar position, then the elbows have flexed too far.

Downward Movement

☐ Lower the bar slowly and under control to the starting position by extending the elbows; do not bounce the bar on the thighs at the bottom position, flex the torso forward, extend the knees, or allow the body's weight to shift toward the toes.

☐ Keep the wrists stiff and the upper arms stationary against the sides of the torso.

☐ Maintain the same stationary body position with the feet flat on the floor.

☐ Continue to lower the bar until the elbows are fully extended but not forcefully locked.

☐ At the completion of the set, slowly flex the hips and knees at the same rate (to keep an erect torso position) to squat down and return the bar to the floor in a controlled manner.

Biceps Curl (Machine)

Starting Position

☐ Before performing this exercise, check the height of the seat and position of the chest pad and adjust them to allow for the following conditions:

■ The thighs are approximately parallel to the floor (with the feet flat or in the foot supports).

■ The torso is perpendicular to the floor when sitting erect with the torso against the chest pad.

■ The lower part of the back of the upper arms and the elbows are pressed against the arm pad.

■ The elbows are in line with the axis of rotation of the machine.

☐ Sit erect with the feet flat on the floor or in the foot supports and press the torso against the chest pad.

☐ Stand up partially and reach forward to grasp the handles with a closed, supinated grip and then reposition the body to achieve the seated erect torso position.

☐ The elbows should be fully extended, the arms parallel to each other, and the elbows in line with the axis of rotation of the machine. All repetitions begin from this position.

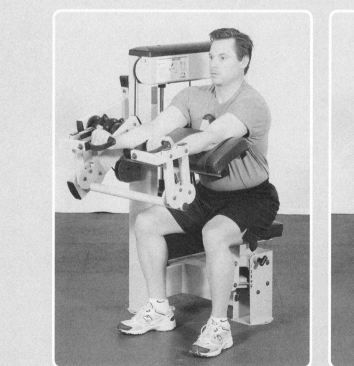

Starting position

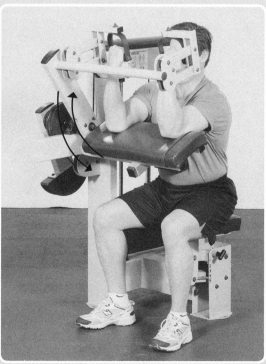

Upward and downward movements

Upward Movement

☐ Begin the exercise by pulling the handles in an arc by flexing the arms at the elbows.

☐ Keep the wrists stiff and the upper arms stationary against the arm pad as the handles are raised; do not let them move forward or outward. No movement should occur at the shoulders; movement should occur only at the elbow joints.

☐ Maintain the same stationary body position; do not quickly lean back farther to help pull the handles.

☐ Continue flexing the elbows until the handles are near the anterior deltoids or until the elbows are flexed approximately 90 degrees (depending on the type of machine). If the elbows lift off the arm pad at the highest handle position, then the elbows have flexed too far.

Downward Movement

☐ Allow the handles to move slowly and under control back to the starting position; do not bounce the forearms on the arm pad at the bottom position or lift the buttocks off the seat.

☐ Keep the wrists stiff and the upper arms stationary against the arm pad.

☐ Maintain the same stationary body position with the feet flat on the floor.

☐ Continue to lower the handles until the elbows are fully extended but not forcefully locked.

☐ At the completion of the set, slowly stand up partially and reach forward to return the handles to the resting position.

Triceps (Single-Joint) Exercises

DVD 2

Name	Description of the concentric action	PREDOMINANT MUSCLES INVOLVED	
		Muscle group or body area	Muscles
✋ Lying barbell triceps extension	Elbow extension	Upper arm (posterior)	Triceps brachii
✋ Seated overhead barbell triceps extension	Same as lying barbell triceps extension		
Triceps pushdown (machine)	Same as lying barbell triceps extension		

✋ Denotes an exercise that requires a spotter.

Lying Barbell Triceps Extension

Starting Position: Lifter

☐ Sit on one end of a flat bench and then lie back so the head rests on the other end of the bench.

☐ Position the head, shoulders, buttocks, and feet to achieve a five-point body-contact position:

    1. Head is placed firmly on the bench.

    2. Shoulders and upper back are placed firmly and evenly on the bench.

    3. Buttocks are placed evenly on the bench.

    4. Right foot is flat on the floor.

    5. Left foot is flat on the floor.

☐ Signal the spotter to pick up the bar off the floor.

☐ Grasp the bar with a closed, pronated grip.

☐ Move the bar to an extended-elbow position above the chest with the forearms parallel to each other. Externally rotate the arms slightly so the elbows point away from the face (toward the knees).

☐ All repetitions begin from this position.

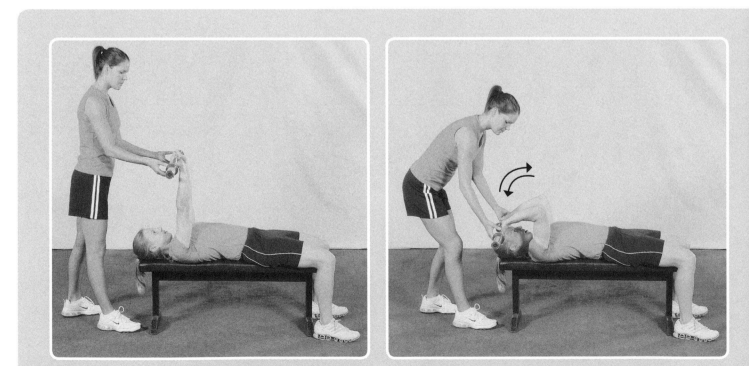

Starting positions   **Downward and upward movements**

Starting Position: Spotter

- ☐ Stand erect behind the head of the bench.
- ☐ Place the feet shoulder-width apart with the knees slightly flexed.
- ☐ Grasp the bar with a closed and alternated grip.
- ☐ Hand the bar to the lifter.
- ☐ Guide the bar to a position over the lifter's chest.
- ☐ Release the bar smoothly.

Downward Movement: Lifter

- ☐ Begin the exercise by lowering the bar in an arc slowly and under control toward the nose, eyes, forehead, or the top of the head, depending on the length of the arms. Lifters with longer arms will lower the bar toward the top of the head and those with shorter arms will lower the bar toward the face.
- ☐ Keep the wrists stiff and the upper arms perpendicular to the floor and parallel to each other. No movement should occur at the shoulder joints; movement should occur only at the elbows.
- ☐ As the elbows begin to flex, they should point toward the feet (not out to the sides).
- ☐ Continue to lower the bar until it almost touches the head or face at its lowest position.
- ☐ Keep the head, torso, hips, and feet in a five-point body-contact position.

**Lowest bar position
(without spotter shown)**

Downward Movement: Spotter

☐ Keep the hands in a supinated grip position close to—but not touching—the bar as it descends.

☐ Slightly flex the knees, hips, and torso and keep the back flat when following the bar.

Upward Movement: Lifter

☐ Press the bar upward under control by extending the elbows back to the starting position. No movement should occur at the shoulder joints; movement should occur only at the elbows.

☐ Keep the upper arms and elbows stationary; they should not move forward or out as the bar rises.

☐ Maintain the same stationary five-point body-contact position; do not arch the low back, raise the hips, or push up with the legs.

☐ Keep the wrists stiff and the upper arms perpendicular to the floor and parallel to each other.

☐ Continue to press the bar up until the elbows are fully extended but not forcefully locked.

☐ At the completion of the set, signal the spotter to take the bar, but keep a firm grip until the spotter gains full control of the bar.

Upward Movement: Spotter

☐ Keep the hands in a supinated grip position close to—but not touching—the bar as it ascends.

☐ Slightly extend the knees, hips, and torso and keep the back flat when following the bar.

☐ At the lifter's signal after the set is completed, stand up and grasp the bar with a closed and alternated grip, take it from the lifter, and set it on the floor.

Seated Overhead Barbell Triceps Extension

Starting Position: Lifter

☐ Grasp the bar evenly with a closed and pronated grip, narrower than shoulder width but not closer than a position where the thumbs, when extended along the bar, could touch each other.

☐ Follow the preparatory body position and lifting guidelines (see introduction) to lift the bar off the floor to a position at the front of the thighs.

☐ Sit on one end of a flat bench, position the feet flat on the floor moderately wider than hip-width apart, and sit erect with the shoulders perpendicular to the bench and the head in a neutral position.

☐ Move the bar to the front of the shoulders.

☐ Signal the spotter for assistance to move the bar to an elbows-extended position over the head with the upper arms next to the ears, parallel to each other and perpendicular to the floor.

☐ Externally rotate the arms slightly so the elbows point away from the face. All repetitions begin from this position.

Starting Position: Spotter

☐ Stand erect and very close behind the lifter. This will require the spotter to straddle the flat bench.

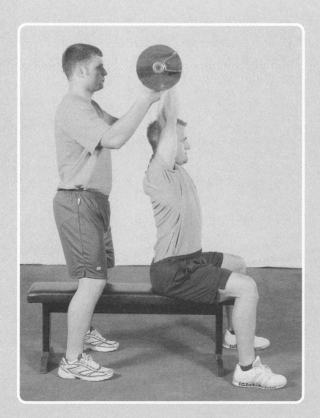

Starting positions

Downward and upward movements

☐ Place the feet shoulder-width apart with the knees slightly flexed.

☐ Grasp the bar with a closed and supinated grip.

☐ Guide the bar to a position over the lifter's head.

☐ Release the bar smoothly.

Downward Movement: Lifter

☐ Begin the exercise by lowering the bar in an arc slowly and under control, bringing it down and behind the head.

☐ Keep the wrists stiff and the upper arms perpendicular to the floor and parallel to each other. No movement should occur at the shoulder joints; movement should occur only at the elbows.

☐ As the elbows begin to flex, they should point away from the face (not out to the sides).

☐ Continue to lower the bar until it almost touches the base of the head or neck (depending on the length of the arms) at its lowest position.

☐ Maintain erect posture with the feet flat while sitting on the end of the bench.

Downward Movement: Spotter

☐ Keep the hands in the supinated grip position close to—but not touching—the bar as it descends.

☐ Keep the knees slightly flexed and the back flat when following the bar.

Upward Movement: Lifter

☐ Press the bar upward under control by extending the elbows back to the starting position. No movement should occur at the shoulder joints; movement should occur only at the elbows.

☐ Keep the upper arms and elbows stationary; they should not move forward or out as the bar rises.

☐ Maintain the same stationary body position; do not move the head, body, or feet as the bar is raised.

☐ Keep the wrists stiff and the upper arms perpendicular to the floor and parallel to each other.

☐ Continue to press the bar up until the elbows are fully extended but not forcefully locked.

☐ At the completion of the set, signal the spotter to take the bar, but keep a firm grip until the spotter gains full control of the bar.

Upward Movement: Spotter

☐ Keep the hands in the supinated grip position close to—but not touching—the bar as it ascends.

☐ Keep the knees slightly flexed and the back flat when following the bar.

☐ At the lifter's signal after the set is completed, grasp the bar with a closed and supinated grip, take it from the lifter, and set it on the bench or the floor.

Triceps Pushdown (Machine)

Starting Position

☐ Stand under a high-pulley station with the torso erect, shoulders held back, back against the vertical back pad (if one is present), head in a neutral position, and eyes focused ahead.

☐ Grasp the bar evenly with a closed, pronated grip, approximately 6 to 12 inches (15 to 30 cm) apart. (Various bar attachments can be used for this exercise; the most common is an 18-inch [46 cm] straight bar.)

☐ A minimum recommended grip width is close enough for the tips of the thumbs to touch each other when they are extended along the bar. A maximum distance is where the forearms are parallel to each other.

☐ Place the feet shoulder- or hip-width apart with the knees slightly flexed and the torso erect.

☐ Pull the bar down to position the upper arms and elbows against the sides of the torso with the forearms parallel to the floor (or slightly above). Do not lean forward or turn the head to position an ear next to the cable; instead, keep the head in a neutral position with the cable directly in front of the nose. The body should be close enough to the machine so the cable hangs nearly perpendicular to the floor when the bar is grasped and held in the starting position.

Starting position   Downward and upward movements

☐ Hold the shoulders back, keep the upper arms and elbows pressed against the sides of the torso, and keep the abdominal muscles somewhat contracted. The selected load should be suspended above the remainder of the weight stack. All repetitions begin from this position.

Downward Movement

☐ Begin the exercise by pushing the bar down by extending the elbows.

☐ Keep the wrists stiff and the upper arms perpendicular to the floor and pressed against the sides of the torso. No movement should occur at the shoulder joints; movement should occur only at the elbows.

☐ Continue to push the bar down until the elbows are fully extended but not forcefully locked.

☐ Maintain an erect torso and slightly flexed knee position; do not squat down slightly, lean forward, move the elbows backward, or move the cable to the right or left to help push the bar down.

Upward Movement

☐ Guide the bar slowly and under control back up to the starting position; do not allow the bar to jerk the arms upward.

☐ Keep the upper arms and elbows stationary; they should not move forward or out as the bar rises.

☐ Maintain the same stationary body position; do not move the head, torso, or feet as the bar is raised.

☐ Keep the wrists stiff and the upper arms perpendicular to the floor and pressed against the sides of the torso.

☐ Continue to guide the bar up until the forearms are parallel to the floor (or slightly higher).

☐ At the completion of the set, slowly guide the bar under control to its resting position.

Forearm (Single-Joint) Exercises

DVD
2

Name	Description of the concentric action	PREDOMINANT MUSCLES INVOLVED	
		Muscle group or body area	Muscles
Wrist curl	Wrist flexion	Forearms	Flexor carpi radialis Flexor carpi ulnaris Palmaris longus
Wrist extension	Wrist extension	Forearms	Extensor carpi radialis brevis Extensor carpi radialis longus Extensor carpi ulnaris

Wrist Curl

Starting Position

☐ Grasp the bar evenly with a closed, supinated grip 8 to 12 inches (20 to 30 cm) apart.

☐ Follow the preparatory body position and lifting guidelines (see introduction) to lift the bar off the floor to a position at the front of the thighs.

☐ Sit on one end of a flat bench and position the feet hip-width apart with the legs parallel to each other and the toes pointing straight ahead. Lean the torso forward to place the elbows and forearms on top of the thighs.

☐ Move the forearms forward until the wrists extend slightly beyond the patellae.

☐ Open the hands, allow the wrists to extend in order to rest the back of the hands on the patellae, and roll the bar down so it is held with curled-up (flexed) fingers. All repetitions begin from this position.

Upward Movement

☐ Begin the exercise by raising the bar by flexing the fingers and then the wrists.

☐ Keep the elbows and forearms stationary; do not jerk the shoulders backward or rise up on the toes to help raise the bar upward.

Starting position

Upward and downward movements

☐ Continue flexing the wrists as far as possible without lifting the wrists off the thighs.

Downward Movement

☐ Lower the bar slowly and under control to the starting position; do not lift the elbows off the thighs.

☐ Maintain the same stationary body and arm positions with the feet flat on the floor.

☐ At the completion of the set, lift the arms off the thighs and slowly lean forward and return the bar to the floor in a controlled manner.

Wrist Extension

Starting Position

☐ Grasp the bar evenly with a closed, pronated grip 8 to 12 inches (20 to 30 cm) apart.

☐ Follow the preparatory body position and lifting guidelines (see introduction) to lift the bar off the floor to a position at the front of the thighs.

☐ Sit on one end of a flat bench and position the feet hip-width apart with the legs parallel to each other and the toes pointing straight ahead. Lean the torso forward to place the elbows and forearms on the top of the thighs.

☐ Move the forearms forward until the wrists extend slightly beyond the patellae.

☐ Keep a closed grip on the bar but allow the wrists to flex completely in order to rest the front of the hands (the knuckles) on the patellae. All repetitions begin from this position.

Upward Movement

☐ Begin the exercise by raising the bar by extending the wrists.

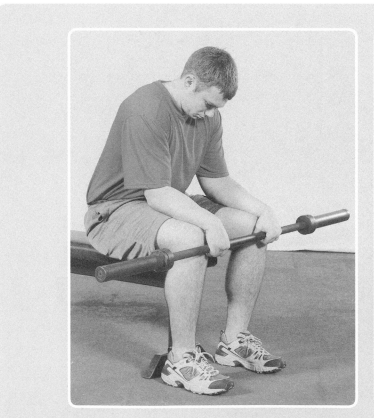

Starting position

Upward and downward movements

☐ Keep the elbows and forearms stationary; do not jerk the shoulders backward or rise up on the toes to help raise the bar upward.

☐ Continue extending the wrists as far as possible without lifting the wrists off the thighs.

Downward Movement

☐ Lower the bar slowly and under control to the starting position; do not lift the elbows off the thighs.

☐ Maintain the same stationary body and arm positions with the feet flat on the floor.

☐ At the completion of the set, lift the arms off the thighs and slowly lean forward and return the bar to the floor in a controlled manner.

UPPER BODY

ABDOMEN

Abdominal Exercises

Name	Description of the concentric action	PREDOMINANT MUSCLES INVOLVED	
		Muscle group or body area	Muscles
Bent-knee sit-up	Trunk flexion	Abdomen	Rectus abdominis
Abdominal crunch	Trunk flexion	Abdomen	Rectus abdominis

Bent-Knee Sit-Up

Starting Position

☐ Lie in a supine position on a floor mat.

☐ Flex the knees to approximately 90 degrees and flex the hips to approximately 45 degrees to place the feet flat on the mat with the heels close to the buttocks. The thighs, knees, and feet should be next to each other.

☐ Fold the arms across the chest or abdomen. All repetitions begin from this position.

Upward Movement

☐ Begin the exercise by flexing the neck to move the chin nearer to (but not touching) the upper chest and then curl the torso to lift the upper back off the mat.

☐ Maintain the same stationary lower-body position with the arms folded across the chest; do not lift the feet off the mat as the upper body is raised.

☐ Continue to curl the torso toward the thighs until the upper back is off the mat and the elbows point toward the thighs.

Downward Movement

☐ Uncurl the torso then extend the neck slowly and under control back to the starting position; do not lift the buttocks off the floor to help rebound for the next repetition.

☐ Maintain the same stationary lower-body position with the arms folded across the chest.

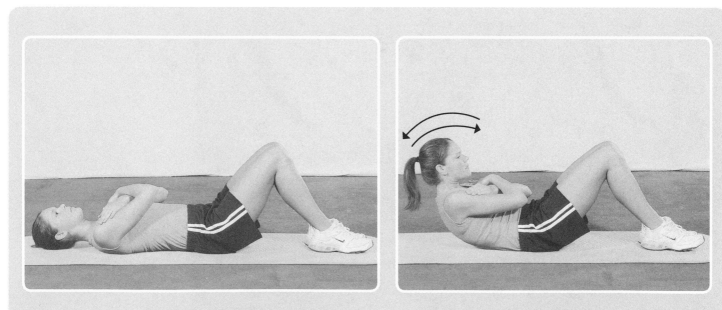

Starting position   **Upward and downward movements**

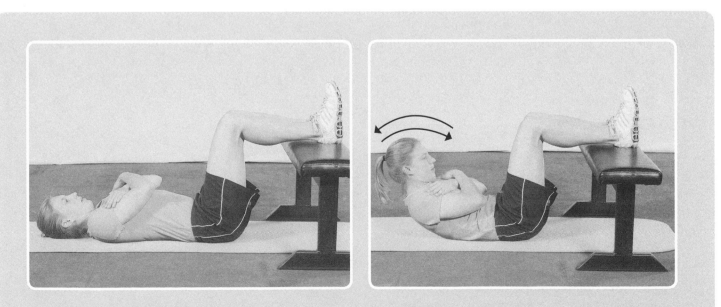

Abdominal Crunch

Starting Position

☐ Lie in a supine position on a floor mat.

☐ Place the feet on a bench with the hips and knees flexed to approximately 90 degrees. The thighs, knees, and feet should be next to each other.

☐ Fold the arms across the chest or abdomen. All repetitions begin from this position.

Upward Movement

☐ Begin the exercise by flexing the neck to move the chin nearer to (but not touching) the upper chest and then curl the torso to lift the upper back off the mat.

☐ Maintain the same stationary lower-body position with the arms folded across the chest; do not lift the feet off the bench as the upper body is raised.

☐ Continue to curl the torso toward the thighs until the upper back is off the mat and the elbows point toward the thighs.

Downward Movement

☐ Uncurl the torso then extend the neck slowly and under control back to the starting position; do not lift the buttocks off the floor to help rebound for the next repetition.

☐ Maintain the same stationary lower-body position with the arms folded across the chest.

Starting position   **Upward and downward movements**

About the NSCA

The National Strength and Conditioning Association (NSCA), a nonprofit educational group, was established in 1978 to generate and disseminate information about strength training and conditioning to its members and the general public. Evolving from a membership of 76 in 1978, it now has more than 30,000 members in over 63 countries, including international chapters in Japan, China, and the United Kingdom. The NSCA is widely recognized as an international clearinghouse for strength training and conditioning research, theories, and practices.

Central to the NSCA's mission is providing a link between the scientist in the laboratory and the practitioner in the field. By working to find practical applications for new findings in strength training and conditioning research, the organization has fostered the development of strength training and conditioning as a discipline and as a professsion.

The NSCA offers two distinctive credentialing programs. The Certified Strength and Conditioning Specialist (CSCS) credential is the certification of choice for professionals who design and implement strength and conditioning programs for athletes, and the NSCA-Certified Personal Trainer (NSCA-CPT) credential is an ideal certification program for those who train active and sedentary clients in one-on-one situations.

The NSCA's prestigious CSCS and NSCA-CPT certifications are the only programs in the fitness industry that have been nationally accredited since 1993 by the National Commission for Certifying Agencies, a nongovernmental, nonprofit agency in Washington, DC, that sets national standards for certifying agencies. To earn one of these internationally recognized certifications, candidates must pass a rigorous exam administered by an independent exam service. To date, more than 35,000 professionals residing in 59 countries hold one or both of the NSCA's credentials.

Join the thousands of strength and conditioning professionals worldwide on the cutting edge of research and practical application. Whether you're a student defining your career path, a coach or trainer looking for more resources, or a seasoned professional, the National Strength and Conditioning Association offers a strong community to help you go further.

Learn more at **NSCA.com.**

TAKE YOUR CAREER FURTHER))))

everyone **stronger**
NSCA.com